Brand Yourself as the Trusted Local Celebrity™:

25 Marketing Strategies to Stand Out as the Obvious Choice in Your Market

Donna Gunter

Orange, TX

Copyright © 2018 by Donna Gunter.

All rights reserved. No part of this publication may be reproduced, distributed or transmitted in any form or by any means, including photocopying, recording, or other electronic or mechanical methods, without the prior written permission of the publisher, except in the case of brief quotations embodied in critical reviews and certain other noncommercial uses permitted by copyright law. For permission requests, write to the publisher, addressed at the address below.

BizSmart Publishing, Orange, TX 77630
https://www.BizSmartPublishing.com

Cover Design © Nathan Dasco, http://nathanieldasco.com

Brand Yourself as the Trusted Local Celebrity™: 25 Marketing Strategies to Stand Out as the Obvious Choice in Your Market/Donna Gunter. -1st ed.

ISBN-13: 9781731342799
ISBN-10: 1-73134-279-9

Dedication

This book is dedicated to my best friend and husband, Eric, who has supported me and encouraged me and believed in me more than I ever imagined....

Table of Contents

Dedication	3
Table of Contents	5
Introduction	7
Bonuses for Readers	10
Leading with Authenticity	11
Get Focused with Your Niche Market	15
Your Killer Thirty-Second Commercial	21
Explode Your Business with Your Trusted Local Celebrity™ Book	25
Your Authority Website	29
Get More Prospects with a Lead Magnet	33
Create an Ezine That Gets Results	37
Take Action Client Testimonials	41
Media Releases That Get Traction	45
More Eyeballs with Content Syndication	49
Expand Your Reach with Content Curation	53
Increase Your Traffic with Guest Blogging	57
"Borrow" Authority by Interviewing Experts	61
WOW! Them with Your Signature Speech	65
Reach More Eyeballs with Video Marketing	69

Leverage Your Expertise with Webinars	73
Reach More People with Slidecasts	77
Speak to Thousands as a Podcast Guest	81
Host Your Own Podcast	85
Monetize Your Expertise with Product Creation	89
Create a Signature System That Attracts Clients Like Crazy!	95
Create Your Dream Team of Influencers	99
Massively Grow Your List with a Virtual Summit	103
Reach More People via Social Networking	107
Networking in Professional Associations	111
Interview with Neil Howe, Co-Owner, Atlanta Eco Cleaners	115
Bonuses for Readers	127
About Donna Gunter	129

Introduction

There are several advantages to being the obvious choice and trusted celebrity for your clients and prospects. Let's begin by defining what a Trusted Local Celebrity™ is. *Merriam-Webster* defines local celebrity as "someone whom everyone in the area knows or recognizes." I tweaked the term a bit to Trusted Local Celebrity™ because it doesn't help if you're recognized for all the wrong reasons. Being recognized as someone people trust is more important to help you grow your business.

In my mind, a Trusted Local Celebrity™ is someone who knows enough to help their customers and prospects with a specific problem and is willing to share that knowledge and is recognized for doing so. I like to think of this as being an educator and advocate for your clients. Wouldn't you find it easier to talk about yourself as an educator and advocate for your clients, rather than the expert?

Please don't misinterpret my use of the word "celebrity." Trust me, as a card-carrying introvert, the last thing I want is the paparazzi circling my driveway every time I leave my home or having to appear on local television at every opportunity (although that local coverage is GREAT for business). I'm not fond of being the center of attention at all. However, if you're out and about and people come up to you and say, "Oh, I recognize you! You're Dr. Sattler, that chiropractor who advertises on Channel 4. I've been meaning to request a copy of your book about pregnancy chiropractic that you mention in the ad," then you've become a Trusted Local Celebrity™. I'm really referring to recognition in small doses to help you build your business. although you can take it to a larger scale if you're an extrovert!

I have experienced this when I go to conferences. When I walk into a room, people come up to me and say, "Oh, you're Donna Gunter! I'm on your email list! I just attended your webinar!" And then they'll start a conversation with me about something I've written or some training I've done, and it takes me a few moments to catch up with what they're talking about. It's very low-key — no flashbulbs, no red carpet – just simple recognition for the education and advocacy I've been putting forth in my marketing.

What led me to create this system? I'm an introvert at heart (INFP on the Myers-Briggs scale) and I HATE to market myself. However, what I discovered is that marketing becomes very easy when you are an educator and advocate for your clients. My Trusted Local Celebrity™ System is completely built around the concept of education-based marketing.

Why would you want to be a Trusted Local Celebrity™?

1. Create business and brand domination. This goes without saying, right? If you think of financial planners, you might immediately think of Suze Orman or David Bach. If you were to think about a medical doctor, Dr. Oz would probably come to mind. Once you've become the obvious choice, you have name recognition when someone thinks of your industry.

2. Gain a huge edge over the competition. There's no doubt about it. If both you and your competition are showing up on the first page of Google for certain search terms, the prize will go to the business that appears to be everywhere, or has several third-party citations, like from affiliates of ABC, NBC, CBS, CNN, or on YouTube or other blog or association sites. No longer is being on the first page of Google enough- you have to demonstrate your expertise once someone has found you.

3. Attract more quality clients who will pay you top dollar for your advice. Once others view you as the authority, your clients will value your advice more and be willing to pay top dollar for it.

4. Open more doors to bigger opportunities. Calls from radio and TV hosts, guest posting on popular blogs, keynoting a speech at a conference, and being asked to write articles for popular trade magazines are a few of the opportunities that will come your way as a highly paid authority.

5. Develop multiple streams of income from sharing your expertise. Multiple profit centers are a great way to leverage your expertise and into books, home study programs, ecourses, and high-end coaching or mentoring programs.

6. Become the hunted rather than the hunter. It's nice when your prospects chase you down to work with them rather than the other way around. Having authority and being the obvious choice lets you stop the client chase once and for all!

7. Create financial freedom where your biggest problem is saying no. When you become the well-known and highly paid authority, it's much easier for you to pick and choose only the work that you truly want to do. And, if the opportunity doesn't fit your needs or your schedule, you can say no without having to worry financially.

Let's begin your journey to becoming a well-known Trusted Local Celebrity™ and obvious choice for your clients.

Bonuses for Readers

As a gift for my readers, I have several bonuses that you can download at https://www.LocalCelebrityBranding.com/.

STRATEGY ONE

Leading with Authenticity

I had lunch several years ago with a colleague in a networking group. We talked about many things and were trying to get to know each other so that each of us could better understand what might make a great referral for the other. One of the things he told me caused me to chuckle because it seemed to surprise him.

He told me that he liked my website because I was straight-forward, to the point and I just "put it all out there." By that he meant that I outlined what I do, how I do it, the benefits of what I do, and that I let the visitor decide to either buy into it or not. Most surprisingly, I didn't seem to have any attachment to the visitor's decision either way. I didn't waste any time trying to convince visitors that I was always the right choice, regardless of circumstance. However, if the visitor does "buy" into what I'm offering, they have ample opportunities to get on one of my lists and/or purchase something from me.

My response to his observation was that, as a small business owner, I had the responsibility of discouraging as many people as possible from wanting to do business with me. I know this philosophy sounds crazy, especially when the gurus tell you to always be selling.

Here's my belief: I'm not out to sell my services or my products to the world, nor do I want to sell my services to everyone. I only work with clients who meet my ideal client profile and only market to those in my target market. Period. And, that's only a very small chunk of the world. Why? Because I truly believe that there's enough business for everyone.

My business and my life are so much more fun and joyful when I work only with clients that I love. I do that through what I call the WYSIWYG approach, or "What You See is What You Get." I am who I am and let that center of authenticity come through in all that I do - my speaking, my writing, my website, my coaching, my personal interactions.

If you don't "buy" into the business that is me, that's wonderful! You can continue your search for a consultant who better meets your needs, and I still have room in my practice for clients with whom I love to work. If you do drink my Kool-Aid®, that is buy into what I do and who I am, you're doing it because on some level, you're buying into "Donna the Person," and the good, bad, and ugly that accompanies that.

Now that I'm firmly entrenched in middle age, I finally feel that I'm fully coming into my own in all aspects of my life, and I have stopped running away from those aspects that I think others might not like or might be offended by. Being myself for a living is so much easier than trying to live up to an image (or create an image) that doesn't really exist.

When working in higher education, I always felt that I was split in two halves, Donna the Human Being and Donna the Housing Administrator. Rarely did the two Donnas meet - they were almost separate personalities, and quite frankly, Donna the Human Being (my true self) didn't really care for Donna the Housing Administrator at all. It's no wonder I felt exhausted all the time in that job - I was living two distinct lives, and one of those lives I really hated. The creation of my own business - and my own set of rules - has freed me to be me - and probably saved me thousands in therapy fees!

My role model in life is the late Ann Richards, former governor of the great state of Texas. Ann was bold, brave, humorous, bright, and embodied the best in a Southern/Texas woman, and made no bones about that. Long ago I decided to embrace my being a "southern girl from the sticks" (English translation-lived in the country in a small East Texas town) rather than trying to make myself over into something more palatable to a wider group.

A former client used to get the biggest kick out of the stories I would tell her about living in a small east Texas town while at the same time telling me I needed to move away from there to a more civilized place. I told her if I moved, she would lose her great source of funny stories that she could incorporate into her speeches, and I would lose what makes me "me."

As a small business owner, how can you incorporate "you" into your business so that your ideal clients are naturally drawn to you? What natural gifts and talents do you possess but aren't willing to acknowledge? I strongly encourage you to tell your story - your parable of why you do what you do. Playing to your gifts and being who you are for a living is an extraordinarily rewarding way to run your business. Most importantly, it's what makes your business distinct - and helps you stand out in a sea of small businesses.

STRATEGY TWO

Get Focused with Your Niche Market

When you are just starting off any business, being a jack of all trades may seem like a good idea, but eventually you will realize that niche market is a far superior alternative. Instead of trying to cater to the entire market, you become a specialist in a very tiny niche. Focusing your efforts on a tiny market segment allows you to master that niche. You become an undisputed expert in your area and your target market recognizes you as one.

Some people may frown at the idea of ignoring large segments of the market and losing potential customers but becoming a niche expert has its advantages. Let's take the example of surgeons. Neurosurgeons see fewer patients than general surgeons, but they are paid many times more because very few doctors can do what they do. They are specialists, but now consider pediatric neurosurgeons. Pediatric neurosurgeons are "super" specialists and operate within a very small niche segment of the market. They are few and their time is booked months in advance. They earn more than most other surgeons.

You can also become an expert in a very small niche market. Specialists are few and competition will be low. People are willing to pay more for specialists, and although your volumes may be low, your revenue and bottom line will always be healthy.

Niches are created by identifying needs, wants, and requirements that are being addressed poorly or not at all by other businesses and then developing and delivering goods or services to satisfy them. To become an expert and reap the benefits of niche market, you must find the right micro-niche on which to focus.

Here are 5 steps to follow to discover your niche market:

Step 1: Determine your industry. This step should be straightforward. Your profession will be the gateway. If you are a lawyer, your industry is legal services. If you are a real estate agent, your industry is real estate. Try not to restrict yourself to a small area within your field in this step because you will be closing out options that may make sense when you consider your knowledge and expertise in those areas.

Step 2: Segment your industry into smaller micro-niches. Now, it's time to break down your field into several smaller segments where specialization is possible. For example, if you are a real estate agent, here are some possibilities:

Real estate -> Buying and selling -> Homes -> Luxury homes -> Penthouses
Real estate -> Buying and selling -> Homes -> Green homes
Real estate -> Buying and selling -> Homes -> Distress sales -> Foreclosures
Real estate -> Buying and selling -> Homes -> Distress sales -> Short sales
Real estate -> Buying and selling -> Homes -> Rent to own

If you have been in the field for some time, it will be easy to come up with many niches. Each area is small, and you will be able to devote sufficient time and energy into any one of them should you choose to become an expert in that market segment. When you have listed all possible niches, the next step is to evaluate them.

Step 3: Evaluate each area. This evaluation helps you analyze each niche area in isolation. You can then decide if it is worth entering and whether you have it in you to become a niche expert.

> **a. Sub-niches or topics**. Analyze each niche. Is there enough complexity in it to make expert help valuable? For example, take buying and selling luxury homes. Is there a need for an expert over there? Possibly. Now take distress sales. Will an expert make a difference here? Definitely yes. There are different kinds of distress sales and many things that can go wrong, which makes expert help valuable.
>
> If you are unsure about a niche, search for it in Google and see what other searches have been made related to the same subjects. You can also use the Google Keyword Tool, which will give you a lot of information about searches related to that topic. A quick look at the contents of books on the topic can also throw some light on the complexities in the niche. Stores like Amazon allow you to check the table of contents of books.
>
> **b. Pain points**: People seek out experts and are willing to pay more for them when they are suffering, and a generalist cannot solve their problems. Look for areas where there is pain. In addition to getting a ready and willing market and being in demand, you will also have the satisfaction of helping people in distress.
>
> Let's take our real estate example again. Is there any pain in buying and selling luxury homes? Possibly not, but they are bought by rich people who will be willing to pay a premium for an expert. What about distress sales? Yes, this is one area where there is a lot of pain and if you become an expert in this area, besides being in

demand, people will be grateful to you for helping them salvage whatever they can.

c. Attainability. Do you have the required expertise in the field? Will you be able to help people solve their problems? If not, you must not pose as an expert, as no one will be fooled. If you have the potential to become an expert, you can work at a slightly higher level in the same segment and then slowly specialize in your chosen area. You can also consider working with another expert and eventually gain the necessary knowledge.

d. Numbers. Does the market have the potential both in terms of numbers and revenues to make entering it worthwhile? You can do some online research and check if people are placing ads to find prospects in this segment. If people are spending money to find customers, you can assume that there is potential in the area. You can also check for discussion forums, blogs and social groups related to the niche to get an idea about the demand.

Step 4: Become the authority and the source of original ideas in your selected niche. Once you have selected your area of specialization, become the innovator for your target market. Publish and share fresh, high-quality content regularly. You can distribute the same content over multiple channels like blog posts, videos, ebooks and SlideShare. If you release fresh content every week, you will become one of the top sources of original content and stay well ahead of your competitors. Look at the market's needs, understand their problems and provide solutions. Do everything you must to position yourself as a top expert.

Step 5: Showcase your content to more people. While most of your content will go into your own web properties, it is also important to publish content through other non-competing channels. Do guest posts. Get yourself interviewed for podcasts and radio shows. Podcasters are always looking for people to interview and with your expertise, it should be easy to be interviewed by a couple of them every month. Eventually, you will be able to graduate to premium media like TV and newspapers.

Instead of trying to cater to large markets and competing with thousands of other people, become an expert in a micro-niche and become a champion in your selected area. You will stand out from the crowd and it will be easy to attract customers. The ease of getting customers and the premium pay you get by niche market will more than compensate for the lack of a large market to which a generalist caters.

Download my free checklist, *Creating Your Target Market Avatar*, at https://www.LocalCelebrityBranding.com/.

STRATEGY THREE

Your Killer Thirty-Second Commercial

Even though your business may be completely Internet-based, there are still numerous times when you need to give your killer thirty-second commercial, also known as an elevator speech, that explains what you do and how you do it. It's called an elevator pitch because it's generally something you could tell someone in an elevator between floors in response to the person's inquiry about what you do. Whether you're a guest on a webinar, hosting a webinar, being interviewed for a radio talk show, creating a podcast, talking to prospective clients on the phone, striking up a conversation with a stranger at the grocery store, or simply writing web copy for your website or blog, you need a clear, concise way to explain your business to others.

I've seen savvy service business owners take this concept to new levels as follows:

1. using their elevator pitches as audio introductions on their websites
2. printing their elevator speech on their business cards
3. creating a movie with audio, graphics and animations that they copy to DVDs or flash drives to send to prospective clients or post on video sites like YouTube

So, even if you don't attend face-to-face networking meetings, which has traditionally been the most commonplace use of an elevator speech, having a ready-made 30-second commercial at your disposal continues to be an important marketing tool that you need to continuously sharpen.

I have a simple template that I use with my clients to build their 30-second commercial. By completing the following sentences, you can create your own elevator speech that will provide a crystal-clear answer to what you do.

1. Do you know how some (the customer you are aiming at)...

2. Experience (the problem)...

3. Which means that (the outcome of the problem)...

4. Well I do/can do is (your job/product/service)...

5. Which means that (the solution)...

6. The benefit of which is (the outcome of the solution)...

7. Would you like to know more?

As an example, here is the elevator speech that I recently helped one of my coaching clients design for her Virtual Assistant practice:

Do you know how some personal and professional coaches do a wonderful job with coaching but feel completely overwhelmed with all the day-to-day administrative details involved in running their businesses...which means that they try to do it all alone and let opportunities and follow-up contacts fall through the cracks, involve themselves in tasks that prevent them from going out and finding new clients, and dig themselves deeper and deeper into a never-ending to-do list. Well, what I do is take over all the administrative headaches that coaches want to get rid of and don't like to do.... which means that I am expertly managing all the day-to-day business operational details from my home office as an independent contractor...the benefit of which is my clients get more energy from working fewer hours, more clients, greater profits, more balanced lives and more passion for their work. Would you like to know more?

Practice makes perfect, so create several versions of your elevator pitch until you find just the right combination that flows effortlessly from your lips, without any stuttering or stammering. A well-crafted 30-second elevator speech is a beautiful tool to have, and you never know where you may get the opportunity to use it!

STRATEGY FOUR

Explode Your Business with Your Trusted Local Celebrity™ Book

There's a new marketing strategy that pops up each day for entrepreneurs. Business owners feel pulled in too many directions and find themselves chasing too many shiny objects. What they fail to see is that there's a proven, very effective marketing method that has stood the test of time and is superb at positioning them as the educator and advocate for their target market.

What is that? Writing a book about your expertise and use that to grow your business. I refer to that as your Trusted Local Celebrity™ book. This is the most effective marketing strategy that can open huge opportunities for your business. Best of all, YOU don't have to write it. You can easily speak your book, be interviewed about your book, or hire a ghostwriter to help you with your book.

Here's how having your own book can explode your business:

1. Ultimate business card. Books are a great marketing tool that allows you to reach out to a wider audience and provide them with a solution to one of their major problems. When you publish a book about your expertise, you can give or sell copies to people during public speaking opportunities or even distribute them online. Books are the business card that lasts -- people will rarely throw away a book. They tend to keep it on their desks or bookshelves and refer to it repeatedly if it successfully helps them solve a major problem. When you give your book to someone, they instantly become pre-sold on you before you open your mouth, and you then become the welcomed guest rather than a pest who is trying to sell yourself or your services.

2. Automatic lead generation. Give a copy of your book to all of your current clients and prospects to begin the lead generation process. When selling or giving your book away, be sure and collect your prospect's information and add that to your database (with permission, of course) so that you can follow up with that prospect in the future. If you are selling your book via a third-party source, like Amazon, add a page at the beginning of your book that offers a valuable follow-up gift (video, audio, checklist, webinar) that goes into more detail about one of the points in your book. Ask readers for their names and email addresses in exchange for your offer.

3. Media darling. Your book serves as a source of quality information for getting quoted in magazines, newspapers, and online blogs. Most radio and television stations and podcasts love having authors as guests on the shows they host. Therefore, a book can provide you with some amazing opportunities for free media exposure, which no other marketing channel can offer.

4. Credibility. Publishing a book provides you with instant expert status. Other people will now view you as an authority on your topic, as there is still a certain aura of respect, awe, and credibility that follows anyone who is a published author. A book will give credence to your expert status, as you knew enough about a topic to publish a book on it.

5. Increased referrals. Customers trust authors who have written a book on their topic of expertise. Writing a book provides you and your business with increased public exposure and credibility. If you are using your book as your business card, give an additional copy or two and ask the recipient to distribute them to others that might need your expertise. This helps to increase the number of referrals for your business.

6. You, the obvious choice. From increasing your brand's visibility to increasing your referrals and improving your customer loyalty, writing a book provides you with an edge over your competition, most of whom (if not all) have not written their own book. The increased credibility also sets you apart from your competition, which will help to make you the obvious choice when a prospect is seeking a solution to the problem that you solve.

7. Cost effective marketing tool. If you are currently doing any print, radio, television or pay-per-click (PPC) advertising, offer a copy of your book as the advertisement's call to action, rather than focusing on selling your products or services in the ad. Your book acts as your long sales letter, business card, display ad and credibility builder, all rolled up into one, and can dramatically increase the both the quantity and quality of leads you collect for your business.

8. Lead as an educator and advocate. Being an educator and an advocate for your clients is much easier than marketing yourself as a product or service. As an entrepreneur, you possess a certain set of skills and knowledge that are unique to you, your business and the problem that you solve. Publishing a one-problem, one-solution book allows you to offer quality information to prospects to help them solve a specific problem and expertly position yourself to your clients.

9. Increased customer retention. By writing a book, you provide your customers with a tangible reminder of who you are. If you are in a business in which someone might forget your name because they don't use your service that often (like a real estate agent, for example), your book will remind your customer to seek you out to do business with you again.

10. Increased revenue. Writing a book helps to increase your marketing opportunities and generate more leads, which increases your revenue. It can also open new additional income streams such as consulting, speaking and product creation opportunities. The new expert status gained from publishing a book also allows you to charge more fees without the risk of losing customers; clients will pay more for an established expert.

Whatever your goal in writing your book, the bottom line is that a book offers quality content that customers crave. It can also increase your marketing opportunities and generate more revenue for your business, thus creating the option for exponential growth.

Download my free *Trusted Local Celebrity Book Organization Checklist*, at https://www.LocalCelebrityBranding.com/.

STRATEGY FIVE

Your Authority Website

One of the most effective client attraction strategies you can create for your business is to develop an authority website. Most websites, even currently, are simple brochure sites, telling visitors who runs the business, what they do, and how to contact them. An authority website, however, is one based on a specific topic. Better yet, search engines love these sites. Because search engines strive to provide the most relevant sites when someone is seeking information on a particular topic, these types of sites are usually found at the top of search engine results.

To find the authority site in your niche or on any particular topic, simply go to a search engine, type in a keyword, and view the top 3 results that appear in the natural (organic, not pay-per-click) results. These are typically the authority sites for the keywords you entered.

Here are ten steps that business owners can follow to create an authority website for their business:

1. Pick a niche. Make your niche as narrow and focused as you possibly can. Perhaps it's professional organizing for home offices or web design for cleaning companies or career coaching for baby boomer women. You get the idea here.

2. Select your keywords. Keywords are the key to being found online, so select yours carefully. Select a niche specific keyword phrase, two secondary keyword phrases, and then search for other related keyword phrases that have a fair amount of traffic but not so much competition. Google AdWords Keyword Planner, https://adwords.google.com/ko/KeywordPlanner/Home, can help you find these keywords. You should end up with 10-15 keyword phrases at this point.

3. Domain. There's still a bit of leverage given in search engine results to domains that contain your primary keyword. Buy a domain name containing your keyword phrase, if you can.

4. Gather content. Now you need to gather all the content you have created related to this niche. This could be articles, blog posts, audio, or video. If you don't yet have content in this niche, you need to create at least ten pieces of content, each of which uses one of the keyword phrases you found in Step 2.

5. Lead generation magnet. Now you need to create your lead generation magnet, or client attraction device, that you can give away on your site in exchange for a visitor's name and email address.

6. Autoresponder follow-up. Create 8-10 follow up autoresponder messages that are sent out over the next three weeks to the people who requested your lead magnet. The goal here is to educate them about what you do or the product that you sell and invite them to purchase from you.

7. Design and navigation. Make your site easy to navigate and professional with a clear call to action. Nothing is worse than visiting a site that looks as though it were designed ten years ago or gives you a confusing array of things to do. Use a simple design with attractive colors, and make sure your call to action (signing up for your lead magnet) is on every single page of your site. I suggest you create a website using WordPress as your content management system and then have your site customized accordingly.

8. Add content. The content you gathered or created in Step 4 can now be uploaded to your site. Be sure that the keyword for each piece of content appears in the content's title, first paragraph, page description and title, and page headline.

9. Content syndication campaign. In order to begin to create inbound links to your sites from high traffic websites, you need to begin to syndicate your content. Create audios, videos, or slide casts and use a syndication service to send out your audio and video content. Break your content into smaller pieces and distribute it as tips via your social media sites.

10. New content. Content is king online, so plan to create one new piece of content each week that is added to your site.

An authority website will help you leverage your expertise in your marketplace. If you create it according to these steps, it will continue to generate leads for your business while your content syndication system continues to drive traffic to your site. Now, you have created an automated marketing machine that will continue to send clients to your business.

Download my free *Authority Website Checklist* at https://www.LocalCelebrityBranding.com/.

STRATEGY SIX

Get More Prospects with a Lead Magnet

One of the quickest ways to build your email marketing list is by creating a lead generation magnet, or what is commonly referred to as an ethical bribe. This free giveaway serves to entice visitors to your site to sign up for your email list because they want to access your solution to their problem proffered in your email list opt-in box.

What are the three most important characteristics of an effective lead magnet? It must provide the solution to at least one of the problems of your target market. Secondly, it must utilize the keywords that your target market might use when seeking this type of solution. Thirdly, your offering must have a high enough perceived value that your visitors would be willing to buy it.

I routinely opt into many lists just to get the lead magnet. More times than not, the giveaway is simply a long reiteration of a problem, with the solution being available for purchase on the website. This is the WRONG way to introduce yourself to prospects. Don't be afraid to share some solutions with your prospects - it's part of developing the Like, Know and Trust factor with them. If you are truly an expert in your field, the info you share for free is only the tip of the iceberg of the variety of solutions you can provide to your prospects.

What is the easiest way to create your own lead magnet? Here are 10 ideas that you can use to package your information into a valuable lead magnet for your website:

1. Audio of a presentation. Hold a webinar on a topic and record it, or simply record a presentation with audio recording software on your computer. An audience isn't necessary for a good recording - it is quality content that is the key.

2. Interview of an expert. Request to interview a noted expert in your target market. Ask the expert questions or pull questions from a pre-assigned list you've been given. Record the interview and have it transcribed to create a giveaway.

3. Special report. A special report is simply a short PDF report that runs between 2-5 pages. You can create this easily by writing an article that's 1500-2000 words. Format it to be easily read and add a bio page and upsell page and your report is complete.

4. Checklist. A checklist is a 1-2-page PDF file that walks someone through a to-do checklist to complete a task. To create a checklist, simple outline the steps required to complete a particular task and insert a checkmark box in front of each so that the user can print out the list and mark off the steps as they are completed.

5. Video. Using video to promote your business is one of the hottest Internet marketing strategies today. You can create an info video that is a training or tutorial video made by using video screen capture software or record using PowerPoint or record yourself answering questions or presenting a topic with an inexpensive webcam, smartphone camera or Google Hangouts. Upload it to your site or to one of the video hosting sites, and you've got a new lead magnet to give away.

6. Software or app. For as little as $50, you can hire a programmer to create a simple piece of software or app to help your prospects automate a task or solve a problem. Another option is to buy a license for some inexpensive software that you can then distribute as you wish.

7. Resources list. Once you have developed a relationship with your prospects, invariably you will get asked to make recommendations for vendors to perform certain tasks. Because this list is valuable in that you have already gone through a number of services to find just the right provider and are thus saving your prospects hundreds of dollars and hours of time, create a list of these providers in a PDF document.

8. Templates. Templates are another time-saving device that prevents your prospects from having to reinvent the wheel. Package together templates you regularly use, like templates for telephone follow-up calls, emails, email newsletters, to-do list, budgets, etc. Anything that will let your prospect use as a model for developing her own version will be greatly appreciated.

9. Worksheet/workbook. Sometimes information is better delivered in a format where the prospect can jot down ideas, answer questions, or brainstorm. A PDF worksheet or workbook is the ideal format for that to happen. Create a document with a series of questions and space to answer the questions, along with a bit of introductory text to set up the question, and you've created a useful workbook.

10. Ecourse. An ecourse is a series of emails that deliver information over a specific course of time via email. Your ecourse can last as short as 3 days or as long as 52 weeks. Once you pick a topic, simply determine the number of points that you want to make as you discuss the topic, and then create an email that thoroughly explains each point. Put the emails together in a sequence in your email marketing program and you have an ecourse.

Download my free report, *17 Ways to Promote Your Lead Magnet*, at https://www.LocalCelebrityBranding.com/.

STRATEGY SEVEN

Create an Ezine That Gets Results

At almost every meeting I attend in my city, I get positive feedback about my ezine, or email newsletter. People generally tell me they love it, or they ask some question about something I've written about in a previous issue. All in all, it's pretty cool--I kinda feel like a celebrity!

In everything that I do, my goal and my focus is to get subscribers to my newsletter list. I don't start out trying to sell them a program or get them to buy some product. I just want them to get my weekly email newsletter. That's it. Just get a little dose of Donna on a weekly basis (pun fully intended).

My rationale behind this comes from my philosophy that people have to know, like, trust and respect you before they'll decide to buy anything from you. I've finally acknowledged and embraced that I'm a pretty good writer and have decided to lead with that gift and use that as my marketing tool for my business.

About 12 years ago, I decided that I made some serious changes to how I published my email newsletter, and I immediately began to see some dramatic changes in client prospect behavior as a result of the writing I do each week. The changes include readers calling or emailing me to sign up for a program, to sit in on a webinar, or to form a strategic alliance with them. Just exactly what I'd hope would happen!

Here are the five secrets to newsletter publishing that I learned through the "school of hard knocks" that have helped successfully market my business through email newsletter publishing:

1. Publish consistently on a weekly basis. I initially published my newsletter on a not-so-regular basis initially because I didn't see my newsletter as a serious marketing tool (silly me!). I then went to a regular monthly publication about a year later and then to a twice-a-month publication, and finally ended up publishing weekly in 2003. Now, if I miss a week, I'll get a couple of emails wanting to know what happened and where the newsletter is.

2. Let your "voice" permeate your newsletter. My first newsletters had some great resources that a busy business owner would find helpful in the management of his/her business. The only thing about me was a short paragraph about my business at the end of the newsletter. What I realized was that the newsletters to which I best responded were those in which I got to know the writer and liked what s/he had to say. Resources were great, but lessons through personal experiences were incredibly more valuable and were the things that I remembered about the newsletter. I definitely put more "me" into my weekly newsletter now.

3. Show how you can help clients solve problems. I could just kick myself for letting almost three years slip away by doing such a slip-shod job in demonstrating my expertise. Again, resources are useful, but stories of what I'm experiencing or what clients have experienced in their businesses and decisions that have been made to change the way we're doing business are much more helpful to my readers. Hence, in every newsletter, there's now a content-rich "how-to" article in each issue to help my readers run a better business.

4. Set aside time to write your newsletter. Finding space in my calendar to set aside time on a weekly basis exclusively for this marketing activity isn't always easy. There are many times I want to fill that time with "profit generating" activities (i.e. work with clients) rather than holding onto this time as a business development activity. Since I now publish weekly, it takes me about 2 hours to write the main article for the newsletter. I now set aside time from 9 AM-noon each Wednesday morning and knock out the newsletter copy. Some weeks the process flows more easily than others.

5. Repackage and re-purpose your articles. One of my primary motivations now for doing my newsletter is that I've now got a personal article bank of roughly 300 articles that I can reuse, tweak or re-purpose when I need to. I publish my weekly ezine article on my website and have it available to use to create a special ebook or report that I can sell as another income stream, or re-purpose as a special report for a giveaway on my website. As a matter of fact, this book is a compilation of articles that I originally wrote for my ezine.

What I've now discovered is that by having this client "reservoir" in place (my email newsletter subscribers with whom I go out and touch base weekly), my marketing has gotten so much easier. On a regular basis, one of my readers will wake up and decide that they've had enough and can't do it this way any longer and decide to hire me.

If you don't currently have a newsletter in place that permits you to reach out and "touch" potential clients regularly, I encourage you to start one. If you currently have an email newsletter, pay more attention to its care and feeding so that it grows a healthy prospective client base for you. It'll be one of the best investments you'll make for your business.

STRATEGY EIGHT

Take Action Client Testimonials

Client testimonials can make or break a website. They are a vital factor in establishing a relationship of trust with new visitors to your site. Visitors want to see that others just like them have hired you or purchased your products and have successfully overcome some hurdle or some issue. Better yet, when the testimonials specifically note how the client's life or business has been enhanced by buying your product or service, the visitor then begins to believe that it will help her overcome a similar issue, as well.

Several years ago, I updated one of my sites. I continued to get phone calls from potential clients who wanted to hire me, but the calls were much different than I had gotten previously. The difference was that I spent the duration of the phone call in sales mode to convince them to hire me, which is something I hate to do. I'd never had to do that before. Usually they were already sold on the concept of hiring me and just wanted to know when we could get started.

I racked my brain to try and figure out what in the world was going on and what had changed with these prospects. Suddenly it hit me that in the update of my site, my client testimonials had gotten lost in the process and weren't on the new site. This gave me the motivation I needed to get additional testimonials from satisfied clients and determine how to best display those testimonials for maximum impact. Once I added those to my new site, things returned to normal and those rave reviews did all my selling for me.

How do you go about getting testimonials that say something more compelling than, "Jane is great to work with"?

Here are ten questions you can ask your clients to get results-oriented client testimonials for your business:

1. What factors made you to choose my business to assist you with <fill in outcome desired by your client here>?

2. What were your preconceived notions about using <my type of business, service, or product>. For example, "What were your perceptions about working with an accountant before we started?"

3. How has that perception changed since you hired me/bought my product?

4. What do you like most about working with me/using the product?

5. Did you expect it would work as well as it did?

6. Did you have any objections/hesitations before you decide to hire us/buy the product? If so, what were they? How did we overcome those?

7. What are the three biggest benefits of working with us/using the product? OR How has your life changed/things changed since you began using our service/product? Please be as specific as possible (i.e. we increased sales by 25% in 3 months; I lost 15 pounds in 20 days; I doubled my income last year).

You may also want to ask this as a before/after question, i.e. "How are things different now after hiring us than they were before you hired us?"

8. If you were to recommend me to a colleague, friend, or business associate, how would you describe the way I provided my service to you (or, the way I helped you achieve a certain result)?

9. Is there anything else you'd like to add that I haven't yet asked about?

10. Can I share this information in our marketing materials?

If you don't have any client testimonials on your site, it's not too late to go out and solicit a few. Use these questions to increase the trust visitors have in your services and products and increase your sales dramatically!

STRATEGY NINE

Media Releases That Get Traction

Media releases, also known as press releases are an inexpensive way to get the word out about your business and build your brand. However, you can make each press release stretch further if you have a plan outside of random distribution.

While you are creating your media release, figure out exactly who you want to see it and write for your target audience, making it easy for the press, as well as your target market, to find you. Then, ensure that your media release has a news-worthy story behind it.

Here's how to write a media release that gets more traction:

1. Add important links. While most links for online press releases are "no follow." still include a link or two to your website and the product or event announcement on your website.

2. Craft compelling headlines. Your headline should evoke curiosity from the reader by answering a question that has been burning for the audience.

3. Repost it on your website. A media release is more content for your website. After submitting it to various affiliates of ABC, NBC, CBS, and major newspapers and radio sites, add it to the Media Room of your website, then send it to your connections.

4. Build relationships. Use media releases to build relationships with your audience and journalists by writing about what your audience wants to know and how they want to learn it.

5. Send to the right people. Don't just blanket press rooms with your release; instead be laser-targeted with who gets the release so that you don't become known as a PR spammer.

6. Include a photo. By including a photo of yourself as a part of your release, you'll increase the likelihood of having your release read.

7. Include a video. Have you produced a video with more details about your story or has a sound bite that the press can use? The awesome thing about digital press releases is that they can include videos or links to videos, providing more information for the press.

8. Include keywords. Using keywords is important in headlines, subtitles and bullets. Be careful about creating keyword links because you want don't want to be accused of keyword stuffing, but you do want to use keywords strategically so that the search engines pick it up.

9. Tell a story. The words inside your press release matter; the story must be important and compelling enough to get readers to not only read but to act on what they read.

10. Share and ask for shares. When you distribute a press release, share it with everyone and ask them to share it too. Don't just rely on the press connections or your PR firm to get the word out about your release.

Press releases are good for building your media page, building relationships, proving expertise and more. They are also good for announcing new products, events and grand openings. But, you have to get in the practice of writing them and distributing them for them to work. Use these tips on how to write a media release to ensure that your release gets the attention it deserves.

Download my free guide, *101 Reasons to Claim Your Authority with a Media Release***, at** https://www.LocalCelebrityBranding.com/

STRATEGY TEN

More Eyeballs with Content Syndication

Content syndication has become one of the most rewarding strategies to build your authority and effectively reach prospective readers or potential customers. The concept of content syndication describes the process of pushing your content out into your own or third-party websites in the form of a full article, snippet, link thumbnail, video, slideshow, or infographic.

When used correctly, content syndication can contribute to building a larger fan base, improving your SEO strategy, increasing your popularity, enhancing your positioning and encouraging sharing of your content via social media platforms.

Here are 10 ways to build your authority with content syndication:

1. Publish in your ezine. Every single article I've ever written has appeared as an article in one of my newsletters. My commitment to publishing a weekly email newsletter forced me to commit to writing a new article each week. I'm not sure I would have honored my commitment to article writing had I not forced myself to produce an email newsletter on a weekly basis.

2. Post to your website. Roughly 60% of my traffic comes to my website via keyword searches that match the topics of blog posts that I've written. I use my blog articles to send both current and prospective clients to my site for additional information on a topic that enhances a recent discussion I've had with them. For maximum usability, index the posts on your website in usable categories that make sense to your target market so that they can easily find your words of expertise when they search for it online.

3. Publish on social media sites. You can't move anywhere online today without running into some social media site -- Facebook, Twitter, LinkedIn, Instagram, etc. Post a link to your article on all the social media sites on which you participate.

4. Create a podcast. Make a digital recording of your article using one of any number of audio recording services like Spreaker, https://www.spreaker.com/ or software like Audacity, https://www.audacityteam.org/. I create a special intro and outro (special offer) for each podcast, based on the content of the article, and then proceed to read and record the text of the article. Then, post your podcast to podcast directories. In about 30 minutes, you've created yet another piece of content syndication for your business.

5. Create a video. Video production is now all the rage. In fact, you can actually sit at your desk or go outside and easily record a video with your smartphone. With the magic of screen capturing software like ScreenFlow or Camtasia, you can add graphics and text and have a video ready in minutes. With the popularity of video sites like YouTube, it's harder to ignore the impact video will have on your online marketing efforts.

6. Write a press release. Distributing a press release online can have a strong impact beyond any media that might pick it up. You can convert your article into a tips release, a release that ties into a current trend or news story or to an upcoming event that you're sponsoring. This strategy takes a bit of work, as you need to modify the content of your article into the press release format and orient it to your goal for publishing the release. I use and highly recommend for online press releases.

7. Create a Slidecast. Slidescasts are another form of content some people really love. You can use PowerPoint, Keynote, or Google Slides to create your slide deck. Each slide should have one key point from your post. These points should be the headers used in your post to define the different sections. For example, a Top 10 list of will have 12 slides – 10 slides with the items from the list and an introduction slide and an ending slide with your contact information. Once you complete the slide deck, upload it to SlideShare, https://www.slideshare.net/.

8. Create a webinar. If you write your article in the tips format, you've got a webinar in the making. All you need to do is create an introduction and closing for your webinar and beef up your tip points with additional explanation or with examples, and before you know it you will have created the content for a 60-minute webinar.

9. Distribute to print publications in your target market. If your target market is very specialized or is a niche market, you'll find a whole host of specialized print magazines, newsletters, and catalogs for this market. Take a few hours and research those publications available for your target market, check out their submission guidelines, and get a sense of the tone of the publication. If you think your content would be a great fit, buff up a couple of your best articles and send an email to the publisher outlining how publishing your content in their publication would benefit their readership. Since you may not be paid for your submission, request that a short bio with your contact info is contained within your article.

10. Create a special report. Want to create a quick giveaway to offer to colleagues as a bonus for their product, or as a giveaway to your contacts? Create a PDF of your article as a special report that includes your contact info, as well as an upsell page to particular products or services. Or, you can make this report a viral marketing piece that is free for others to give away.

Don't let your content sit on your desktop gathering dust. Put them to work for you by creating a syndication plan to help you get the most out of your content.

STRATEGY ELEVEN

Expand Your Reach with Content Curation

There's a new marketing sheriff in town, and her name is content curation. I've been reading about this process for the last six months or so, and since it seems to be gaining in popularity, I thought the process was worth a deeper look. Content curation is the process of finding, assembling and presenting interesting and up-to-date information on a certain subject. It is rapidly gaining popularity with bloggers and companies that rely on Internet marketing and content marketing, in particular.

However, content curation is very different from content marketing. While content marketing revolves around the creation of new content, the content curation process involves looking for relevant information about a certain subject, enhancing the curated content with additional ideas, feedback, and your own take about the matter, and then passing the curated information on to your readers. Most often this happens on a blog.

Although the term is relatively new to many, it is highly likely that you have used a form of curation in the past. Content curation can take the form of blog links, online news mash-up, social media feeds, RSS feeds, pictures, videos and songs among other digital content. The act of curation is practiced on a number of well-known blogs, like

Mashable.com and HuffingtonPost.com.

The benefit to you as the blogger is that you get to serve as the information filter to your followers by finding the best content for your niche and making sense of what you find in a manner that helps your readers become aware of the most important activities going on in and around any niche. You, then, become known as a go-to expert in your industry without really creating any new content yourself.

Here are seven proven ways to use content curation to be seen as the go-to person in your industry:

1. Videos. You can gather a diverse collection of relevant videos on a particular topic for your readers. This is even made simpler by the fact that most video websites allow permit embedding of their videos. As you curate these videos, you need to write a short introduction detailing reasons why readers should watch the video and what they will get out of them.

2. Expert Tips. As an expert in your industry, you can create a valuable list of the tips on a specific topic in your industry just by pulling the various tips from other experts into a comprehensive guide. Then, aggregate these tips into a list for a valuable piece of curated content.

3. Social Media. Social media is a great place to find quality and informative content, which you can save in a document and then push the content out to your social networks. How often do you retweet or repost something you like out to your list? When you do so, you're practicing basic content curation. However, you should ensure that the content is useful to your followers. And, be sure that all of your social network accounts have a common profile name and are interlinked so that your fans and followers will recognize you regardless of the platform that you use.

4. Infographics. Infographics are images that display information like data, copy, or both, presented in an easy-to-digest visual manner. If you've noticed some cool infographics in your industry, include them in a blog post and share your thoughts about them. See a great infographic on the topic of content curation here.

5. Book list. How about creating a list of relevant books for your readers? You can add a short review to each of these books, and then update the list regularly to ensure that return visitors would always find new information. You can easily include ebooks in this list, as well. If you're an Amazon affiliate, you can increase your revenue by using affiliate links in your list.

6. Resource page. Content curation makes it easy to offer large collections of information, like a resource page or section. To make it user-friendly, create an easy-to-navigate resource page that contains links to relevant content on the topic of the resource. Enhance that page by including your own information on the topic.

7. Case studies. I love to learn by example, and I bet you do, too. And, real-life examples provide great social proof. So, if you want to emphasize or possible disprove an idea, pull together some case study examples from others that support or refute your point.

Content curation is not simply the act of posting the information that you find online. Rather, content curation helps you plan and execute a strategy that distinguishes your activities from those of your competitors, addresses the needs of your target market, and helps you become the go-to expert in your industry.

STRATEGY TWELVE

Increase Your Traffic with Guest Blogging

One traffic generation strategy that I'm started to explore is that of guest blogging. Guest blogging is the process of looking for other blogs read by your target market where you can submit your content for publication. This strategy is a natural fit for anyone who is using content marketing as a traffic generation strategy, as it provides yet another opportunity to syndicate your content to a hungry market looking for the information that you provide.

However, there's more guest blogging than just throwing blog posts here and there in a haphazard fashion. How do you go about finding guest blogging opportunities that will really pay off for your business?

Here are 7 steps to guest blogging your way to more traffic and increased online visibility:

1. Find possible guest blogs. Create a list of blogs that you read where you would like your content to appear. You can also search for blogs on Blog Search Engine, http://www.blogsearchengine.org/. Peter Sandeen has a great list of blogs that accept blog posts http://www.petersandeen.com/list-of-guest-blogging-sites/, and you can track your posts, as well as search for blogs that accept post with Guest Post Tracker, https://www.guestposttracker.com/.

2. Research the blogs. Use a tool like Alexa Traffic Rank for Chrome, https://chrome.google.com/webstore/detail/alexa-traffic-rank/cknebhggccemgcnbidipinkifmmegdel?hl=en, to ensure that the blog is getting some regular traffic. Take a look at the blog, as well, to make sure that the owner is updating the blog with new posts weekly. Read several of the blog posts to get a feel for how the blog owner writes, and look through the categories and posts to see if your content would be a good fit, as well as to determine if your content would fill a missing gap in that blog.

3. Research submission criteria. Many blog owners will note on a page in the blog what they require for guest posting, like only taking original articles, restricting the re-posting of submitted content to other online sources, requiring a set word count, etc. Be sure that you can live with the criteria outlined on the blog before taking any additional steps. If there are no submission criteria, contact the blog owner and ask about his guest blogging policies.

4. Prepare post. Now that you have found a blog or two that will accept your guest post, it's time to get your content ready for submission. Make sure that you have created a compelling headline, have your resource box ready with a call to action that will drive traffic back to your site, and determine the anchor text in your blog that you want to use to create backlinks to your site. Anchor text are hyperlinked keywords that link back to your website. So, for example, if you wanted to rank for "marketing consultant," you would need to use some variation of that term in your resource box and in your content, with that term hyperlinked back to a page on your website.

5. Contact blog owner. If you are "cold calling" a blog owner to guest post, prepare a short introductory email that explains who you are; why you'd like to be a guest blogger (remember your research in step #2);

information about your credentials, writing experience, and your own blog traffic; as well as your post idea. Go ahead and attach your post, as well, so that the blog owner can gauge its appropriateness for his blog.

6. Promote the post. If your post is accepted for the guest blog, show your appreciation by helping promote the posts. Make a mention of the post in your ezine or blog or post a status update on your social networks to drive your friends and followers to that post.

7. Follow-up for future posts. If all goes well in your initial guest blogging gig, ask the blog owner about returning as a blog guest, or even about blogging on a regular basis. Determine the conditions of your follow-up posts, and then follow through on those conditions. You've created the beginning of a beautiful relationship!

Guest blogging can bring you more traffic, more subscribers, and greater online visibility for your business and your brand.

STRATEGY THIRTEEN

"Borrow" Authority by Interviewing Experts

Many service professionals wonder how they will ever become known in their industry, given the easy access to the abundance of information found online. Almost everyone claims to be an expert, so it stands to reason that some percentage of that group are charlatans. How do you create trust and authenticity with your target market and be seen as a real, true expert rather than as a sham?

One of the easiest and quickest ways to do this is by interviewing experts in your industry. People pay big bucks to listen to or meet people like Mark Victor Hansen, Richard Branson, and Bill Gates. While these people may be considered celebrities in their fields, there are celebrity-caliber experts in every industry that members of that industry would be eager to hear speak and would gladly pay for that privilege.

What's nice about this strategy is that the "celebrity factor" of interviewing experts rubs off on you, as you then become the person who knows "Miss Big Name" in your industry because you just interviewed that person. And, if you use the interviews as a lead generation strategy, you name is getting out to thousands in your target market in a big way.

Here are the 10 steps you can follow to help you become your industry's leading expert in 30 days by conducting expert interviews:

1. Research your industry leaders and compelling topics. Off the top of your head, you can probably easily list 10-20 leading professionals in your industry. And, given your level of expertise, you can also probably list 3-5 of the most compelling topics or problems in your industry. Create a list of your experts and topical areas and note which are experts in what areas. Note their email addresses or phone numbers where they can be contacted.

2. Narrow your focus. Once you've taken a look at the experts and the current topical areas of interest in your industry, create a focus for your interviews. Perhaps you choose online marketing for chiropractors, lead generation strategies for real estate agents, publicity techniques for speakers or new retirement options for baby boomers. Whatever your focus, make sure that your grouping of interviews has an easily identifiable theme that will resonate with your target market.

3. Create your list of your top 5-10 favorites. Take your list and organize it from most favorite to least favorite speaker. Create a goal of 7 speakers to interview and begin working the list.

4 Create a web page featuring your speakers. Before you begin contacting your speakers, create a web page featuring your top 10 speakers and their speaking topic. This is something you can show to your invited speakers to give them a sense of who else is being invited and/or has accepted your interview invitation. To remain ethical, you need to note on that page which of the speakers are confirmed and which are still in negotiations.

5. Invite them to be interviewed. You can begin with an email invitation, but as many of those are easily overlooked or are simply not delivered, getting on the phone and calling the expert is probably your best bet. You'll need to tell them whether or not the interview will be live or recorded, have them sign an agreement that both of you can do what you like with the interview (sell it or give it away), and set your interview date and time.

6. Create your list of questions or ask them for a program outline. Some of your speakers may have a prepared signature speech and a description of that speech. If so, ask them to add the 3-5 things that someone will take away as a result of listening to the interview. This will help you create copy for the interview web page. If they don't have a signature speech, create a list of questions to send them on the topic on which they're being interviewed.

7. Conduct and record the interview. Use a teleconference bridge line or recording system to conduct and record the interview. Most interviews are 60 minutes, which is usually more than enough time for an expert to make several valuable points.

8. Transcribe the audio and edit the audio. Whether you're selling or giving away the interviews, having the audio edited will make life easier on your listeners. Learn how to use audio editing software to balance out the speakers, edit out any hums or background noise, and to add introductory music and outgoing music to the beginning and ending of the audio. And, because some people prefer to read rather than to listen to audio, have the audios transcribed as well.

9. Create a package. Once the interviews are complete and are edited and transcribed, you need to decide about packaging and pricing. You can decide to offer the package of interviews in an electronic format only, as a physical CD/print product, or both, and you can sell the package or give it away. Whatever the way you decide to package them, you need to have a graphic designed to represent the package. If you choose to ship as a physical product, you'll need to have a CD cover and label designed and determine how you're going to duplicate and ship the physical product.

10. Interview the expert a second time and offer the package. In your original conversation with your speaker, mention that you want to conduct two interviews of that speaker - one as a part of the series you're creating, and a second interview promoted exclusively to her list. In the interview for her list, your upsell becomes the package, and your speaker has been set up as an affiliate and earns a commission off of any of the packages sold in that promotion. You've created a win-win situation for both you and your speaker.

Interviewing experts in your industry is a quick way to become a well-known expert to your target market. And, if you choose to sell the package of interviews, you can earn some quick cash, as well. Begin to leverage your expertise by interviewing industry experts, and watch your online business grow!

Download my free list, *Interview Questions to Ask Experts and Influencers***, at**
https://www.LocalCelebrityBranding.com/

STRATEGY FOURTEEN

WOW! Them with Your Signature Speech

I love being a guest on other people's webinars and podcasts. What I love best is the fact that all I must do is show up and talk when someone else is sponsoring them. I'm responsible for none of the marketing and promotion and registration involved with sponsoring a webinar. Best of all is that I don't have to schlep all over town to do these guest speaking gigs. I'm presenting my expertise to my target market from the comfort of my own home office.

How can you add a signature speech to your marketing mix? Here's my 10-step process for creating and profiting from your own signature speech:

1. Create 3 info-packed 50-minute speeches. Have at your disposal at least 3 information-packed signature speeches that you can present at a moment's notice. So many of the webinars that I have attended recently are nothing but thinly disguised sales pitches for a very expensive live event, product, or mentoring/coaching program. I don't object to being sold to - after all, I'm a business owner and I realize that others can't simply give away their time at no charge solely for the joy of doing a presentation. However, what I do resent is wasting my time listening to 45 minutes of sales pitch and 5 minutes of questionably valuable information. Ensure your listeners great value each time that you present and provide information that they use today in their businesses.

2. Craft your description and learning bullet points. Write a one-paragraph overview of your program and include 3-7 bullet points outlining what the participants will learn as a result of participating in your event. Your host will love you, as you've just provided the bulk of the text she'll need to market your program.

3. Write your bio and have your headshot available. Hosts like to begin with a short introduction of the guest and often post the guest bio to their websites or send it out as a part of the event promotion to their lists. In this version of your bio, craft a succinct description of who you are and what you do that includes any certifications you may hold, authorship of books, and your unique selling proposition. Then provide a very short overview of your background and your current company. The goal is to have a short, compelling bio (around 150 words) that takes the host about 20 seconds to read to introduce you. Include a small version of your headshot and logo to help your host add graphical interest to the event promotions.

4. Determine your call to action/sales pitch. Prior to the call, determine your most desired action from the participants. Is it to buy a particular product? Sign up for a complimentary consultation? Send for your free gift and be added to your newsletter list? Ideally, you should offer participants the ability to buy into your business at 3 levels: free, low-cost, more expensive. You'll then have a wider appeal to the audience to capture them at wherever they are in terms of price point. Include your call to action in the promotional emails as appropriate, in your handout, and within your PowerPoint slides. In order to create a sense of urgency, you should set a deadline that falls 24-48 hours after your presentation that serves as the cutoff point for your special pricing offer. If participants are encouraged to register even if they can't participate on the live call (i.e. all registrants can access a recording of the call), create a special offer available only to those on the live class to increase live participation numbers.

5. Create a landing page on your website for participants. If your call to action involves special pricing on your product or service, create a landing page on your website that greets the participants by name, i.e. Welcome XYZ Conference Participants. Customize your page several more times to refer to the participants by name and be sure to include the deadline for the special pricing offer in the text of the page as well as in the P.S. of your sales page. I simply take my traditional sales page and customize it for the group for which I'll be speaking and update the deadlines for special pricing.

6. Design a PowerPoint slide deck and handouts. Even if I'm doing an event with no visual component, I still put together a PowerPoint file of my presentation. I provide that to the host if I'm doing a webinar or presenting in an audio conference room. For webinars, I turn my PowerPoint file into a PDF that serves as a handout for the participants. I add a first page that contains my contact information as well as resources mentioned during the call and my call to action. Talk to your host to determine if she will be distributing the handout via email or on her website prior to the call or if you need to have it available for download from your website.

7. Determine your guesting requirements. When I'm a guest presenter, at a minimum I request a recording of the event that I can use in whatever way I want in my business. I may place it on my site as a free download, send it out as a podcast, make it a members-only benefit, or sell it or include it as a part of another product available on my site. If the host is providing a transcript of the session, request a copy of that as well to use in your business. Lastly, inquire if the host is sending out a follow-up email to participants after your presentation. If so, ask to have your contact info and special offer sent to them again.

8. Research venues offering webinars and podcasts and request to be a guest. Most of the invitations I've received to be a webinar and podcast guest have resulted from articles I've written in professional and trade publications, from someone visiting the speaking page of my website, or from having been heard speaking to another group. However, don't wait for people to contact you. Start to research companies sponsoring webinars, podcasts or workshops for your target market and ask to be a guest. In your request, be sure and provide detailed info about the topic on which you'll be speaking, as well as a copy of your handout. You want to make it as easy as possible for the host to pick you as the next guest.

9. Repackage your speech for different markets. You don't have to reinvent the wheel every time you speak to a different target market. With a few changes in your materials, you can usually change the focus of your presentation and make it appear customized for the target market to whom you'll be speaking. Many times just changing the title and inserting the name of your target market is all you have to do to create a seemingly customized presentation.

10. Ask for a testimonial to add to your website. Once you've completed your presentation, don't forget to ask for a testimonial from your host that you can place on your website. In order to be valuable to you, the testimonial should include info about how much value you provided in the presentation, sample of positive feedback from participants, or how your presentation enabled some type of change or ability to take action from the participants.

Spend a few hours designing your signature speech and begin to offer to present it to various groups. You'll see your both your list and sales numbers grow from this easy-to-implement marketing strategy.

Download my free workbook, *Your Signature Speech Workbook*, at https://www.LocalCelebrityBranding.com/

STRATEGY FIFTEEN

Reach More Eyeballs with Video Marketing

Are you a business owner looking for different ways in which you can use video marketing help in your authority positioning? Many service professionals are seeking ways that will help them better position themselves as authorities in their industry. One of the most effective tools you can use is video. You cannot ignore the power of audio/visuals in getting your message across, especially in this day and age.

Unfortunately, not everyone is able to conceptualize an idea and make a good video about it. I'm frequently asked for some guidance on how business owners can best accomplish video marketing. The most common question that I get is, "What kind of video should I make?"

I reply by giving them this guide containing 8 types of video to help with authority positioning:

1. Slideshows. You do not need to have a deep knowledge about videos to create a great slideshow. All you need is to go to an image site, find and purchase photos that you feel are useful in getting your point across, and then compile them to form a slideshow. You can add some background music or text to spice it up, and your video will be ready for your customers to view.

2. Text video. You can use PowerPoint text slides to make a video that is solely text-based. The text needs to be large enough so that the viewers do not strain their eyes when viewing it. This kind of video can be used to highlight some facts about your business that cannot be relayed in photo form. Of course, you can always incorporate background music and other effects to make it interesting.

3. Cartoon-based video. Who said you cannot have fun while making your video? You can inject some humor for your viewers to enjoy by making a video using animated characters and cartoon figures. It is a very catchy way to get your message across. If you happen to have a company mascot, you can use it to create the cartoon videos.

4. Demonstration video. If you want to demonstrate something for your viewers, then it is best to produce a demo video It is an easy way to show a process, and to ensure that your viewers understand all the important details by showing them exactly what you mean. To make the most effective demo video, you should compile a list of your frequently asked questions, and from there, you can come up with a "how to' video and share it with them. This demo video could be a screen share video if you need to demonstrate how to use a program or a piece of software, and it's a great authority positioning piece.

5. Tour video. Another way you can do your video marketing is by creating a tour around your premises, or even your home office, if you work from home. This is particularly important for those in the service industry like hotels, hospitals, restaurants and the like. Give them a tour around your premises by shooting a video of unique features you want them to see and take note of.

6. Interview-based video. If you want your viewers to get to know you and how you can best help them, then you can do an interview video. Come up with a list of questions that you'd like to answer, find someone to interview you, and then record filming the interview session. These questions can cover you experience, qualifications, values, and other important issues. A really easy way to do this is by using Google Hangouts, which will both record the interview and automatically post it on YouTube for you.

7. Client testimonial video. If your clients are happy with your products and services, then you can request them to help you do a video to share their experience in doing business with you. You can have a series of clients delivering their testimonials, then you edit them and arrange them to make a video collage.

8. Article video. If you have been in business for a while, then you probably have many articles and blog posts that you have written. You can transfer the text of these articles to a PowerPoint presentation, along with some accompanying illustrations, and then record yourself in PowerPoint as you read through your article. Simply export the recording, and you have a great informative video to use on your site. It's a great way to both entertain and educate your clients.

Video marketing allows you to interact with your clients and prospects at a different level. They will get to like, know and trust you, and it gives you the opportunity to share a lot of information while still catching their interest. Video marketing is a great strategy that every business owner should consider to enhance your authority positioning.

STRATEGY SIXTEEN

Leverage Your Expertise with Webinars

I first became acquainted with teleclasses back in 1997 when I stumbled across the coaching community. At the time, I lived in small town in western Massachusetts, and professional development opportunities were few and far between without a 60-75-mile drive to Albany, NY, or to Springfield or Boston, MA.

With teleclasses, I thought I'd hit the personal development motherload. I could simply dial a teleconference bridge line from the comfort of my own home and connected with 10-150 other people around the globe, who were all gathered on a call to learn more about a particular topic. Moreover, in many cases the class was free or low-cost, and I didn't have to get dressed, drive anywhere, find and pay for parking, nor stay overnight, all of which I would have to do if it were an in-person seminar or conference. What could be simpler?

The traditional teleclass has gone by the wayside and has been replaced with webinars, in which a presenter is teaching something by sharing or screen or a webcam via video. Webinars are a great way for people to get a "taste" of what you have to offer without any great expenditure.

Many self-employed service professionals use free webinars as a marketing tool so that participants can get to know them, or as an introduction to a fee-based course/program that they're selling. Instead of dealing with the hassles entailed in putting on a live event, such as finding a venue, arranging for parking, setting up catering and AV needs, and promoting the event, you can provide nearly an identical experience with much less trouble and much less up-front cost.

How do you create your webinar? Here's a list of questions you can use to help you design your webinar. This list of questions will save you time in the webinar design process as well as help you structure your webinar to be as effective as possible.

1. Title: Does it include the topic, who it's for and the outcomes/benefits of a person taking the webinar?

2. What is your intention for hosting the webinar?

3. What are the 5 things you most want your participants to know about your topic?

4. What are the 3 things you want your participants to know about your experience in this area?

5. What are the 5 questions you'll be asking to get their attention and to generate discussion?

6. What are the 5 most common problems that people have in this area?

7. Why is your topic relevant?

8. What will you say to someone who doesn't 'get it'?

9. What trends/facts do you have to support your opinions/topic?

10. What, specifically, do you feel that people should do or do differently, in this area?

11. What steps or strategies have you seen work to make these changes?

12. What relevant stories or examples do you plan to share to illustrate a specific point?

13. Is there a distinction to be made that would help the student understand your topic better?

14. What other information would be helpful to your participants?

Now that you've built it, how do you host it? There are several options out there, ranging from free to expensive, but the one I recommend is Instant Teleseminar, https://www.bizsmartmedia.com/its. Out of all the platforms that I have used, this tried-and-true favorite has never let me down. The only two downsides to this platform are that you cannot export your webcast as video nor can you offer a webcast on replay. However, you can embed the replay of the webcast on a page of your site, and the platforms replay function works with audio only.

Next comes promotion of your webinar to get participants. You'll need to promote your webinar event just like you might do a live event--send out press releases, buy advertising like Facebook ads, sent notices out to your email newsletter or list, have friends and colleagues notify everyone on their lists, post about it to social media and share to social media groups, as appropriate.

Webinars are a very inexpensive way to expand your market reach throughout the world. Pick a subject, invite your contacts, and get started today!

Download my free *Easy Webinar Checklist* at https://www.LocalCelebrityBranding.com/

STRATEGY SEVENTEEN

Reach More People with Slidecasts

I've recently discovered one content marketing strategy that will get your business found in the search engines is through the creation of a slide show, or slidecast, and posting that on slide sharing sites. More and more when I do a search for a term, some of the top results are slidecasts in which the titles match my search phrase. I don't mind looking at slidecasts, as most of the time I can click forward through them quickly and pick up the information that I need, unlike watching a video, where I'm unable to fast forward to get to the "meat" of the video.

If you're regularly creating content, whether that's an article or a blog post, you can easily convert that content into a slidecast.

Here are 7 steps to creating an irresistible slidecast presentation:

1. Brand your slides. Create a template or slide master for your slides that incorporates your logo and your look. You'll want your slideshows to be recognizable as uniquely yours.

2. Create valuable content. It should go without saying that the content for the slidecast should contain actionable content. Don't create a promotional slidecast; rather create one that solves a pressing problem of your target market.

3. Create your Word document. In Microsoft Word, open the article that you will turn into a slidecast. Make sure each sentence of the article is on its own line in the document and then save the document.

4. Import into PowerPoint. Click on "File >> Send To >> PowerPoint". When you use the "Send To" feature, you will notice that the PowerPoint slides aren't properly formatted. Simply click on the top slide in the left hand "slides" view, and then on your keyboard, click "CTRL + A" to select all the slides. Right click on the slides and then select "Slide layout". Select the first slide layout template. This will now turn all the content in the slides into headers and center the content in each slide. Or, choose your new master template, if you created one in Step #1.

5. Format your slides. To make the slides look more professional, insert your "call-to-action" URL at the bottom of each slide so that the viewer will know where to go for additional information. The URL may be that of your opt-in page, a product page, or the home page of your site. You need to determine the appropriate call to action for each slidecast as well as the purpose of the slidecast - whether that is to build your list, sell a product, add subscribers to your blog, etc.

Then, using copyright-free images, add images to each of the slides that matches the content of the slide. You don't need to illustrate each slide with an image, just the ones where it makes sense to have an image. Once you have added the images, you will need to go through each slide and make sure everything fits and flows well. You may need to adjust font size as well as text and image positions. Save your presentation.

6. Create your call to action. In your last slide, you will want to create an effective call to action. Consequently, that means that the last slide is dedicated to telling the viewer exactly where to get more information and how to get there.

7. Upload your slides. There are a number of slide sharing sites online. Create an account at those where you want to post your slideshow, upload your slides, and share them via your social media profiles.

After submitted several slideshows to sites like LinkedIn's SlideShare, https://www.slideshare.net/, you'll soon notice that you have followers on the various slide sharing sites. Integrate this content marketing strategy into your regular online marketing mix to help increase your online visibility and get found online.

STRATEGY EIGHTEEN

Speak to Thousands as a Podcast Guest

What's old is new again. Even though podcasting made its debut in 2004, the shiny new strategy's glow faded in the subsequent years. However, in 2014, podcasting made a resurgence and is now stronger than ever. When I heard the statistic about how by 2016 fifty percent of the new cars are going to have Internet connectivity and the ability to download podcasts, I started paying attention.

I then discovered that one-in-four podcast consumers plug their MP3 players or their smartphones into the car audio systems. I later read that Apple has surpassed 1 billion subscriptions for podcast via iTunes. These were my signs that I needed to jump on the podcast bandwagon.

Because I live in a small town in Southeast Texas, I don't get the opportunity to go out that much and do speaking because I'm three hours from a major city. Podcasting offers me a great opportunity to speak to thousands in my target market from my home in just 30 minutes a week. Being a podcast guest helps you reach a whole new stream of prospects and clients, get your message out there, and add another layer of credibility to what you do.

If podcasting is so great, why not start your own, rather than appearing as a guest on other people's podcasts? Starting a podcast is not for the faint of heart. They take much work to get started, and you must continually feed the podcast. You're constantly on the search to find new guests to interview and transcribing the show notes for each episode as well as syndicating each episode can be time-consuming.

I liken being a guest on a podcast versus hosting your own podcast to having a neighbor with a great swimming pool. You might want your own swimming pool, but then you look at the neighbor's pool and say, "Wow, he's already got a swimming pool, and I really don't have the $40,000 to install my own. Why don't I just go borrow my neighbor's pool?" It's the same thing with a podcast. Why go to all this trouble to start up a podcast when you can be a guest on someone else's?

If you have a geographically-based business such as a chiropractor practice or small business accountant, why should you be on a podcast that is syndicated to people throughout the world? It's about attracting people from all over the globe. It's about establishing authority and credibility among your current geographic customers within your local area. Moreover, you can embed the podcast on your website and send out a link to your email list so that they have the opportunity to listen to what you said on the podcast.

The only people for whom podcasting might not be the best choice are those who are desperate for immediate sales or anyone who's chasing a transaction. Podcasts are evergreen. For that reason, you don't want to promote a time-limited offer, like a webinar that's happening on a certain day or a sale lasts three days. The evergreen factor means you never know when somebody is going to listen to a podcast. They may listen to it right away when it's released, or they may listen to it 3 months, 6 months, 9 months, or even 3 years down the road.

With all the podcasts that are available, how do you decide which ones to select and request to be a guest? Firstly, the podcast needs to be listened to by your target market and needs to be on a topic on which you're an authority. For example, I find a very popular Prepper Podcast that covers different apocalyptic survival strategies. I would have absolutely nothing to contribute to that podcast. Nobody on survivalist podcast wants to know how to be a podcast guest. They want to know what the latest, greatest water filtration system is, or the newest light-weight tent that they can use in case of an apocalyptic event.

Secondly, ensure that the podcast has regularly-scheduled guests without any major gaps in episodes, such as publishing episodes for one month and then there's a three-month absence of any guests, then they come back for a week, then there's another three-month absence. Thirdly, look for hosts who have podcasting experience, with at least 10 episodes published. Ensure that the latest episode was within the last two weeks because that gives you a good indication that they're producing podcasts regularly.

The easiest way to find a podcast on which you can be interviewed is by going to Google and type in "Podcast + <your industry>. When you do that, you'll see multiple listings of podcasts about those particular topics. Simply begin to review and evaluate your findings, and whether they pass your personal litmus test.

When you're pitching yourself as a podcast guest, don't make the mistake of pitching yourself with a vague label without any point, direction, or point of view. You really do have to have a compelling topic and a compelling title that hosts cannot resist. What podcast hosts care about is whether or not you have a topic that's going to be valuable to their audiences and is going to help them in some way.

Turbocharge your Trusted Local Celebrity™ positioning by being a guest on podcasts today!

Download my free guide, ***Be the Guest EVERYONE Wants to Interview,*** **at** https://www.LocalCelebrityBranding.com/

STRATEGY NINETEEN

Host Your Own Podcast

Listening to podcasts isn't something I enjoy or take time for, quite frankly. I'm a visual learner and prefer to read something rather than listen to it, as I find reading a much quicker way to gather the info that I need. However, with the proliferation of audio listening devices, like the whole iPod family and other mp3 players, I must acknowledge that I'm in the minority, I believe. The world is listening to a wide variety of audio files, much more so than ever before in history, and I need to get on the bandwagon or be lost in the dust.

What is a podcast, anyway? A podcast is an audio file that you create in .mp3 format that is uploaded with an RSS (Really Simple Syndication) file to your server for your target market to download on any number of programs created to receive or subscribe to your audio file so that they can listen to it at their leisure on their computer or a personal mp3 device.

Why should you create a podcast? I think it serves as a marketing tool for the solo service professional, who might want to do one of the following:

- create an Internet radio show or talk show in which you create content-rich broadcasts for your target market
- conduct a webinar series in which you interview experts who have solutions to problems faced by your target market
- promote a printed book, ebook, or CD/DVD series by releasing promotional snippets to a wider audience
- provide short and valuable expert tips to your target market

Many podcasts are 30-60 minutes in length, especially when they consist of recordings of radio shows or webinars. However, I think that the listening threshold for most people is about 10 minutes. So, that means that your podcast needs to be 10 minutes or less in length. If it's longer, you really have to grab their attention in the first 10 minutes to keep them listening for the full amount of time.

Good content and a good speaking voice are key to maintaining interest. Don't make your podcast one long advertisement for your services or products -- share some useful information with your target market to help them solve their problems. And, you need to have a good speaking voice. Nothing is worse than listening to someone read a speech with a monotone delivery. So, for maximum impact when you record your podcast (especially if you're just recording yourself), get up and walk around, smile, gesture, or do whatever you normally do when you deliver a speech. Modulate your voice, much in the same way that you would when you have a 1:1 conversation with someone -- put feeling and emotion into your words. I pretend like I'm talking to my best friend, and that helps me with a lively delivery.

What are the steps to creating a podcast?

1. Listen to a few podcasts to get a feel for what others are doing. To listen, you'll need a pod catcher (podcast reader), which permits you to subscribe to podcasts in the same way you subscribe to blogs. I favor iTunes as my podcatcher of choice, which is a free online download. You'll also need to find podcasts, and the quickest way to do that is via podcast directories like PodSearch, https://podsearch.com. To find others, simply search online for "podcast directory."

2. Plan your podcast. Who is your target market? What do they want to listen to? How will your podcast be unique from others in your industry? What's your format (interview others or record yourself)? How long will your podcast be? How frequently will you deliver your podcasts?

3. Podcast Art. You'll want to create "album art" for your podcast, or a graphic representation that many podcatchers upload with the mp3 file. Album art must be a .jpg or .png file and needs to minimally be 1400 x 1400 pixels up to 3000 x 3000 pixels. Any graphic designer can help you create this graphics file.

4. Record your podcast. Many people choose to record their podcast with a free piece of software called Audacity, https://www.audacityteam.org/. It has an easy learning curve and advanced features for more experienced podcasters. Mac users might want to check out Garage Band. For best recording sound, don't use the microphone that came with your computer or that is built into your laptop. You'll want to get a more professional one, such as the ones offered at Plantronics or Radio Shack.

5. Save and upload your podcast to your podcast host. Once you've created your podcast in an mp3 file, I recommend you use one of the many podcasting hosting services available. The problem with uploading it to your website is that audio files are space hogs, and you can quickly exhaust all the storage capacity of your hosting account, not to mention your monthly bandwidth capacity if your podcast is popular and is downloaded frequently. That's why I use a fee-based audio service hosting company, Spreaker, which offers me generous storage and bandwidth capacity for a monthly.

6. Publish and promote your podcast. If you use a podcasting hosting service, the service will publish your podcast and notify various podcast directories about the availability of your new podcast. Or, you can enter the info directly into the major podcast directories. You'll also want to promote the podcast on your website, blog, and in your email newsletter.

One of the easiest ways to do this is to add feed subscription buttons (called chiclets) to your sites. You'll have to cut and paste the HTML code into your templates to create the chiclets. You can get directions on how to publish subscription buttons from the podcasts you want to feature.

7. Make money from your podcast. Advertising on podcasts is still new, but a company like Midroll, http://www.midroll.com/, is a great place to start. Another option is to seek sponsors for your podcasts, just like you would for a radio show.

Don't let the audio world pass you by! Podcasting is a very inexpensive way of helping you get the word out about what you do and what you offer to the world.

STRATEGY TWENTY

Monetize Your Expertise with Product Creation

The creation of your first info product is a huge first step toward implementing multiple streams of income in your business. It means that you have something to sell prospective customers to "size you up" as they consider purchasing your services, that you can sell something 24-7 from your website that demonstrates your expertise, and that you're well on your way to creating a passive revenue stream for your business.

Your process doesn't have to be as detailed as I've outlined here, but if you want to do a thorough job in the creation process, I suggest that you embark on all the steps.

1. Solution to a Problem. The best-selling information products provide a direct solution to a major problem of your target market. If you're a professional organizer, the problem might be how to clean and store and organize holiday decorations so that they can be easily found and used from year to year. If you're a weight loss coach, the problem might be how to stay motivated when you've hit a weight loss plateau. Jot down some of the primary problems of your target market and the process by which you help your clients resolve these issues.

2. Determine Your Offering. Info products come in all types of formats, from ebooks to ecourses to recorded webinars to podcasts to special reports to CD and DVD sets. Take stock of your target market and determine what format would best fit their lifestyle. Are they virtual business owners who work from home at their computers for most of the day? Then an ebook or ecourse would probably work well for this group. Are they busy executives who travel frequently? Then you might consider a portable audio format. You can also combine formats to appeal to a variety of learning styles or lifestyles.

And, of course, cost is a major consideration. Do you want to create a physical product that has to be shipped, or would an electronic download work? There are much greater costs on your end to produce a physical product than an electronic one, and you also have to deal with product fulfillment as well if you choose to sell a physical product. I tell my clients to start with an electronic version and test it out, and if it's successful, move to a physical product, which has greater perceived value in the eyes of consumers.

3. Pricing. Pricing of info products is all over the map. Check out your competition (yes, there will be competing products on the same topic aimed at the same target market) and see what they're charging. You also need to look at your contact database and make some assessments of the value of your information to them as well as what you think they will pay. You can survey your database to determine this info or base it on comparable offerings in the marketplace. Many times, my clients get hung up on the notion of comparing pricing for their info product to what they can find in the local bookstore. Generally, pricing for info products is higher than retail bookstores because the info being sold online is specialized for a target market and is delivered immediately upon order (if it's an electronic download).

The pricing strategy that also seems to sell better online is ending your price with a 7, like in $17, $47, etc. If you offer a high-priced product, consider offering payment via an installment plan, where you charge a bit more each month for the product than if someone were to pay for the product in full at time of purchase.

4. Technology. Do you have the technology in place to create and deliver your offering? If it's an ebook, you'll need either a PDF writer program or ebook compiler software. For an audio program you'll need a microphone and audio recording and editing capabilities. For an ecourse you'll need either autoresponder software or a direct to desktop solution. For delivery you'll need a shopping cart that can deliver electronic products or take shipping info for physical products as well as some type of merchant account to take credit and process credit cards. You'll also want a sequential autoresponder service to follow up with your buyers.

5. Create the Product. This is typically the most labor-intensive part of the process, as you're actively recording or writing or videotaping your information for the product. Some products are easier to create than others, especially if you're recycling other content that you have into a new product. If you're starting from scratch, however, give yourself a full 3-6 weeks of steady work time for product creation. After creating the product, you may want to have it proofread and/or edited in some fashion by a proofreader or an audio/video expert.

6. Graphics. A picture tells a thousand words, and more importantly, info products sell better when the visitor has a graphic representation of this intangible info product item. If graphic design isn't your specialty, find someone to design an ebook cover or podcast album art for you. You may want to have the designer also create a website header banner for the product that you can use on your sales page. You can generally have both done for around $200. The more professional your image, the better-perceived value your product has.

7. Domain, Hosting, and Website. I believe that each info product should have its own domain name and sales page to be most effective. Domain names are inexpensive, so you could actually buy several for each product -- one that reflects the product name, for example, and one that reflects the result someone will receive after using your product. You can use the various domain names and websites for a variety of testing purposes as you go to sell your product. If your plan to create multiple info products, you'll probably want to obtain a website hosting account that will enable you to host multiple domains from the same account. Another option is to forward your product's domain name to a "hidden" page of your primary site.

8. Copywriting. There is a specific formula to copywriting for one-page sales letter websites. The best way to get ideas for your sales letter is to create a Marketing Swipe file of other sales copy that you like. From your swipe file look at the headlines, the introduction, the sub-headlines, the listing of benefits, the product description, the outline of the features, the call to action (request to buy), the closing, and the postscripts. You'll begin to see a pattern emerge when you look at 4-5 sample sales pages.

9. Shopping Cart. Once your product is complete, you need to upload the product into your shopping cart and set up the cart for purchases. This may mean that you also need to set up shipping and handling charges for physical products and integrate your shopping with your shipper of choice. If your state requires the collection of state sales taxes, you'll need to integrate that as well.

10. Follow-up Autoresponders. Creating a series of autoresponders to follow-up with a customer after purchase enables you to stay in front of the customer and reminder her about your other product/service offerings. Design a series of 3-5 autoresponders that will be sent out after a purchase to check in with your customer and tell her the next step she needs to take after her purchase. This might mean referring her to another info product, asking her to join some type of subscription service, or experiencing your service with a free trial.

11. Capturing Contact Info. Sadly, not everyone who visits your website will buy what you're selling. However, you can still capture their contact info by creating a free giveaway for those who may not be ready to buy. This might be a special report or free ecourse, and you follow the same steps outlined previously for creating this giveaway. You'll also need to create 3-5 follow-up autoresponders here as well that will ultimately offer them your product once again.

12. Publish and Promote. Now, you're ready to sell. Publish your website and begin to promote your offering to your own database. You can create a buzz about your product by writing a press release, offering a free webinar, buying ads on other websites or in other newsletters, publishing articles, creating podcasts, purchasing pay-per-click advertising, requesting colleagues to send out notices to their contact lists, and creating an affiliate program in which others can sell your product for a commission.

Creating your first info product can be a time-consuming process. However, once it's created, you stand to earn income from it for years to come. Start to expand your business offerings today with information products.

STRATEGY TWENTY-ONE

Create a Signature System That Attracts Clients Like Crazy!

If you teach what you know in some way (as a speaker, author, coach, trainer, or consultant), you'll soon discover that no one buys training, consulting or coaching. They buy a solution to their problems. So, rather than trying to sell your service (a group coaching package, for example), sell a signature program system that helps your target market achieve measurable results.

What's a signature system? It's a way of putting together a package of what you offer in a step-by-step system that makes your process more easily understood by your target market. Your system helps promote trust in your business because your prospect can more readily understand what you do when you spell it out for them and thus make it easier for them to decide to work with you.

When you create a system of how you work with your clients, you create a higher perceived value with your service, as systems connote that you're sharing an "insider secret" on how something is accomplished as opposed to selling an individual service. A signature program also helps you build your brand awareness in a way that is easily understood by your target market and is easily explained by them when they speak about their experience with you to their friends and colleagues (new prospects). Lastly, you make life much easier for yourself with a system in place because you now have a simple way of describing what you do, and you have created a base foundation of content that you can then develop into multiple profit centers, all based around your signature system.

Here are the 5 steps to follow to help you create your own signature system:

1. Outline your approach. Think about the process you go through when you work 1:1 with your clients. I bet that you've created a way of working with them that is similar from person to person. Jot down the 5-10 processes that you take each of your clients through during the course of your work with them.

2. Determine results. What does your client get out of the process of working with you? If you don't know, be sure and ask your clients. A system has to have an end result in mind that is produced upon completion, so note the kinds of results a client will experience and how their life or business will be different after completing your system.

3. Create your catchy name. The name of your system should hook your target market's attention immediately. Typically, you will want to incorporate the major result experienced by your clients as the name of the program. For example, author and coach Michael Port's signature system is the Book Yourself Solid program. Doesn't every service professional want to be booked solid in her practice?

4. Devise the steps. Take another look at your approach outline and refine your approach into a set number of steps. Typically, 5-10 steps are most effective, as anything more looks too difficult and overwhelming for most people, and anything less is looked upon with some degree of skepticism as not being broad enough to work effectively.

5. Brainstorm the spin-offs. Once you've got your signature system in place, then look for ways to break it down into smaller parts and sell access to those smaller parts. Perhaps each of your steps might make sense as a stand-alone module, or a combination of 2 or 3 of the steps would get a prospect on track toward her goal. No longer do you have to keep creating new programs and services. Everything you do comes forth as a part of your signature system.

If you don't market your business with a signature system, stop now and incorporate this process into your business model. A signature system will make your marketing so much easier, help you help more people with your expertise, and enable you to create multiple streams of income on your way to creating a prosperous business.

STRATEGY TWENTY-TWO

Create Your Dream Team of Influencers

When I first became familiar with the professional coaching industry in the late 1990's, I quickly became a follower of Thomas Leonard, credited with founding the coaching industry as we know it today. One of the suggestions that Thomas offered for growing a new business was to develop a Team 100 List. To complete this list, you were required to brainstorm the names of 100 business owners in various industries with whom you were acquainted who would be willing to help you promote your business, send you referrals, etc. The goal was to share this list with all your Team 100 members so that you all became ardent referrers of each other's businesses.

As an introvert, I always found this task overwhelming. One, I didn't know that many people across all those industries. I might be able to fill out a fourth of the list on a good day. Two, having to go out and connect with the other 75% to complete the list was never going to rise to the top of my To-Do List because connecting with others doesn't come easily for me. In fact, I often find the notion quite nauseating.

However, as a business owner, I've come to realize that it's not what I know but rather who I know that will determine my success. Trust me, as an introvert, that is a bitter pill to swallow, as we tend to value knowledge over relationships. The reality is that proactively reaching out to marketing partners will create business opportunities that you will otherwise miss.

So, how could I accomplish this same objective but use my introverted strengths? Here's how introverts can get referrals and more clients from the top 20 influencers in their industry.

1. Create a manageable list. To prevent overwhelm, create a list limited to 10-20 of the top people in your industry with whom you want to develop a relationship. These are people you don't currently know, but who have the capability of being able to make strong referrals for you to your ideal client or endorse you in some way. Your list might include members of the media, prospective clients, association leaders, industry-leading decision makers, or anyone else you want to include.

2. Keep the list in front of you. Make sure your list is visible to you at all times, whether it is tacked to the wall next to your desk, sits on your computer as a desktop wallpaper, or is visible as a file on your cell phone. By doing this, your list stays top-of-mind at all times. And, if you come up short of 20 influencers, this action will make you take notice of other potential influencers you can add to the list.

3. Get contact info. You can use both online and offline contact methods, so gather the following info for each contact: email address, social networking profile info, blog URL, and snail mail address. Add this info to your contact list.

4. Determine your reach out strategy. Now that you have your list, how and why are you going to contact the person? You could:

- send an email commenting on something you like on their website
- mail a card offering congratulations on a recent accomplishment
- post a thoughtful response to one of their recent blog posts
- retweet or comment on a social networking update

- respond by email to something that you found interesting in a recent ezine issue

Remember, this is all about making a personal connection. Reach out to your list members in a way that is genuine and authentic for you.

5. Start reaching out daily. Each day reach out to the top person on your list. Once you've completed this, move that person to the bottom of your list, and the #2 person then becomes your new #1. The next day, reach out to your new #1, and then move that person to the bottom of your list. In this way, you'll continue to rotate through your list, reaching out to each person once every 30 days or so. In order for this strategy to work for you, it is imperative that you become disciplined and follow through on this task every day.

Look upon your Team 20 list as your "Dream Team" of influencers who could have significant impact on your business through their advice, introductions, and referrals. Follow this strategy daily, increase your sphere of influencers, and watch your client list grow!

STRATEGY TWENTY-THREE

Massively Grow Your List with a Virtual Summit

I've been listening to several list building and lead generation webinars lately, and many of them have been offered in the form of a telesummit. A telesummit is a virtual online conference that offers a line-up of varied speakers over a period, like a few days or over several weeks. The telesummit is usually organized by a theme, like outsourcing or lead generation, or for a target market, like the online telesummit for virtual assistants for which I was recently a guest speaker.

Participation in many of these telesummits requires you to pay a registration fee, but the model you see frequently is the "free for live" model in which registrants can participate in the "live" version of the program, but if they're not able to be on the call live, the only way that they can access the content is to pay a registration fee for the audio file and PDF transcripts.

What I love about telesummits is that they are perfect for a downturned economy. There's no airline reservation to make, no hotel to book, no clothes to pack, no shuttle fees to pay, no bad hotel food to endure.... it's simply conducted from the convenience of your home, the home of your speakers, and the home of your participants. You offer high value with low cost -- a great combination!

In my opinion, this type of event is a genius way to turbocharge your business. Here are 5 secrets to turbocharging your online business with a telesummit:

1. Grows your list fast. Many telesummit hosts report that holding a telesummit has helped them grow their list from 2,000 to 10,000 or 15,000 or greater in a span of only a few weeks when the participants are required to give their name and email address to get the telesummit call-in information. Best of all, the additions to the host's email list are perfect leads for their target market. How did this happen? Because the host carefully chose their speakers who market products and services to a similar target market and created a telesummit around an issue or theme important to their target market. And, in an ideal world, the speaker has a large list and agrees to help market the telesummit to that list.

2. Establishes you as the preeminent expert. When you hold an event featuring well-known speakers, you suddenly become the authority, or the expert in the field. After all, how else could you have attracted these experts if you were not an expert yourself?

3. Helps you open the door for valuable joint ventures (JVs) and strategic alliances. Once you've invited someone to be a guest on your telesummit, you have provided a great service to them by introducing them to others who may not have previously heard of them. And, if you offered some healthy affiliate commissions for telesummit upgrades, they love you because you've helped them make money without a lot of effort. Assuming that your event was a success and there were no major hiccups in the process, this success has paved the way for future joint ventures and strategic alliances with this person. This certainly beats cold-calling someone to try and speak to them to sell them on a JV proposal, doesn't it?

4. Increases your credibility. Another key factor in hosting a telesummit is that the notoriety of your speakers rubs off on you as the host. One of the quickest ways to go from "no-name" to "big name" in your industry is to invite the industry experts to speak at your telesummit. The fact that you now have a connection with the movers and shakers in your industry gives you a leg up boosting your own credibility and expertise in the industry.

5. Makes some cash in the process. In addition to the advantages listed previously, there are a several ways to make a little money in this free telesummit model. First, you offer every participant the ability to "upgrade" to get all the recordings and transcripts of the telesummit. Creating a price increase deadline (before summit vs after summit pricing) may encourage more participants to buy. Secondly, once the telesummit is complete, you can go back to your speakers and offer to interview them a second time exclusively for members of their list. The upsell in this second interview is the complete telesummit recordings and transcripts, on which you pay them a healthy commission on all packages sold.

Examine your business model and see how well a telesummit fits into the mix. You'll need to begin planning 8-10 weeks in advance, but once you see the results, you may want to make your telesummit an annual event.

STRATEGY TWENTY-FOUR

Reach More People via Social Networking

It appears everywhere I turn I'm bombarded with information about some aspect of social networking -- Facebook, LinkedIn, Twitter, Instagram, Pinterest...the list goes on and on.

Based on my use and evaluation of several of these platforms over the last few years, here's my synopsis of the 3 primary social networking sites important for online business owners: Facebook, LinkedIn, and Twitter:

Facebook: This one is currently the most popular, with many people conducting webinars and coaching programs on how to best use it. I do like its clean interface and easy-to-read profiles. Many people, from all demographics, seem to be on Facebook. The service offers the ability to add friends by searching for high school/college classmates and by searching former/current colleagues in the workplace. The downside to the application is that you must have a Facebook account in order to view anyone's profile. More and more plug-ins (small applications) are being added to Facebook every day that tweak how this application functions. If you're an author or a business owner, Facebook permits you to add stand-alone pages about your business(es) or book(s) to your profile. Lastly, if you blog, you can plug your blog feed into your profile to update your friends from your blog every time you make a new post.

LinkedIn: This has been the steady, reliable, social networking platform that's very career and job-focused. If your target market consists of corporate types, this is probably the social networking platform for you. You can add connections in the same way that Facebook provides, and your connections have the ability to submit a recommendation about you if they wish.

Twitter: I still find Twitter the most annoying of all the social networking sites, but's insanely popular with the Millennials, so if that is your target market, Twitter is the place to be!

If your business relies heavily on images for marketing, you might check out Pinterest or Instagram, as well.

Here's what I have learned along the way to make social networking a successful marketing strategy for your business:

1. Pick one platform. So many business owners spread themselves too thin by participating in several social networking sites. I've discovered that you could easily devote your entire day to this endeavor and never accomplish anything else. Pick the best platform that will get you in front of your target market and stick to it.

2. Determine your objective. How does this social networking task fit into your overall marketing strategy? What's your objective -- to sell more info products, to grow your list, to develop joint venture or strategic alliance partners? Determine your goal and remain focused on that goal in all that you do when spending your time to work your platform.

3. Work the platform. No marketing strategy will succeed unless you pay attention to it. In order to successfully use social networking, you need to work your platform every single day. Ideally, this means devoting 30-60 minutes each day on activities like seeking new friends/connections/, commenting on other people's profiles, updating your own profile, and notifying your connections about your current activities.

4. Be patient. Rome wasn't built in a day, and you won't see results of your efforts in a day, either. This is a slow and steady process, much the same way that face-to-face networking is. You've got to be out there building relationships and helping others before you're going to see your social networking goals realized.

5. Invite others. Don't hide the fact that you're playing in the social networking arena -- invite your contacts to play along with you. Most platforms offer you the ability to send out these invitations from your contact database. Let your ezine subscribers and blog readers know as well -- never pass up an opportunity to get to know your contacts.

Pick your favorite social media platform and spend 15-30 minutes a day making connections. You'll be amazed at how many valuable contacts you develop in a short period of time!

STRATEGY TWENTY-FIVE

Networking in Professional Associations

When I lived in a larger city than I do now, I must admit I went nuts in terms of going all-out to participate in a variety of professional associations. I had some experience with most of the groups that I visited in other places I had lived or had clients who had positive experiences with certain groups. I was so eager to become involved again in professional associations that instead of really paying attention to the composition of the group as it existed in the city where I lived, I made decisions to join groups based on my past experiences and experiences of clients.

After a few months (and about $1500 in dues paid), I realized I had made a grave mistake. I knew I had failed to keep in mind a few essential strategies as I evaluated my membership in various groups as a way to build my business.

Here's what I learned:

1. Determine your professional association dues budget for the year before joining anything. I foolishly just kept paying membership dues, without giving consideration as to the total picture of what I'd spent in dues for the year. Set your spending limits and stick to those and in a year evaluate if it's worth your time and money to continue participating in the group.

2. Assess the true amount of time you have available to fully participate in a group. As I was thinking about going to group meetings, I only factored in the actual monthly meeting--not the networking time, not the committee time, not the special event time. You may determine that you have much less time than you think.

3. Make sure the target market of your business is represented in the group. I joined one group thinking that it would be full of women business owners, as that had been my experience elsewhere. The local chapter was filled with women who were happily employed for someone else--not a good match for my needs in terms of building my business.

4. Visit the group the maximum number of times you are permitted to do so as a guest. Instead of doing this, I based my joining decision on one visit and impressions of the group I had gleaned from other areas of the country. You really need to assess whether this group in this location will meet your needs, as each chapter within an association can be dramatically different. The local members really do make or break a group.

5. Set your intention of your outcome before you decide to join the group. Are you joining to socialize, to find a date, get industry-specific education, meet other business people, or to build business relationships and make sales? Having a clear goal and focus and evaluating those goals in terms of realistically achieving those in the group should factor into your decision-making process.

6. Acknowledge that it might take you a year or more -- in the right group -- to build the trust others need to have in order to do business with you. Don't expect to walk into a group of people who do not know you and expect them to buy what you're selling or to enter into a joint venture with you. They have to get to know, like, and respect you before they're interested in doing business with you.

7. If you decide to join a group, you need to join a committee or two to get to know the membership. Simply showing up once or twice a month to a meeting will not help you get to know the other members of the group. It is at the committee level where the real networking occurs and where you will develop deeper relationships with other members of your association.

8. Ensure that the groups you join don't have essentially the same membership. It may be different in larger cities, but in my case, I saw the same faces again and again at certain events and meetings. If you belong to multiple groups with a similar membership roster, your time and money would probably be better spent diversifying your professional association memberships.

9. Is your industry over-represented in the group? I've attended some meetings of groups that were full of real estate agents or financial planners, and the group wasn't a professional association of either industry. Make sure your group is well-balanced in terms of member industries and that there is room within the group for someone from your industry to join without stepping on toes.

10. Only participate in groups that meet at a time of day when you're at your best. If you're not an early morning person, those "rise and shine" breakfast meetings probably won't work for you. Several groups I joined met during lunch, and I discovered that the middle of the day is the most difficult time for me to get away. Consequently, I've reduced the number of groups to which I belong who have lunchtime meetings, as that's just not convenient for me.

Joining professional associations can be a very powerful tool for growing your business, if approached with forethought and planning.

CASE STUDY

Interview with Neil Howe, Co-Owner, Atlanta Eco Cleaners

Neil Howe and his wife, Amanda, started Atlanta Eco Cleaners as a part-time job when they moved back to Atlanta, Georgia, from Destin, Florida, after the Deep Horizon oil spill in 2011.

They quickly found a hungry market in the cleaning industry for an all non-toxic and eco-friendly cleaning service. Neil, a veteran in SEO (Search Engine Optimization) was able to lift the cleaning website to the top of the search engine results page and got quite a bit of business right away that turned the part-time cleaning business into a full-time company.

Atlanta Eco Cleaners stayed a family business, but quickly became a six-figure business shortly after introducing authority marketing strategies, which had a huge impact on the marketing and advertising of the business and reputation.

Neil continued to market the business and saw the opportunity to offer marketing services to other businesses in the house cleaning industry. His wife, Amanda, ran the day-to-day operations at Atlanta Eco Cleaners. He and Amanda have now sold the business.

Neil, take us back to the time in your business before you had used any authority positioning strategies. How were you getting clients? How was your business? What was happening in your business at that point in time?

Neil Howe: Let me give you a quick back story. I was in SEO (Search Engine Optimization). I've been doing SEO for a number of years until a big algorithm shift in 2011 where everything changed. The big Google Panda and Penguin updates cost me a bunch of customers in that business.

We were living kind of large then on the beach and a nice big house when I lost a lot of customers basically overnight. We had to make some quick changes. We decided to cut our losses and move back to Atlanta partially because of the Deepwater Horizon oil spill was right on the Florida Gulf Coast. So the oil spill happened right around the same time as the Google update, which devastated that area, and that's where my main client base was. Things didn't go well there from a marketing perspective, so we decided to move back up to Atlanta where it's a bigger city and we could get some business going there.

In the meantime, my wife told me she going to see if she could do something to get another income started. Her idea was to start a cleaning business, and I agreed with her choice, as it doesn't take a great deal to start a residential cleaning business. All you need is a website, some flyers, maybe a few hundred dollars' worth of equipment and you're good to go. That is how we got started. It wasn't really planned. It was a kind of spur-of-the-moment decision.

So, I said, "Well, I know a little bit about SEO so let me do a website." We got the website up and we started getting some customers. We were a bit of a mess with the first few customers that we had. We were standing and staring at each other, not really knowing what to do. We were going into people's houses. When you're used to cleaning your own house, it's fine, but when you go into somebody else's and you've got to deal with all their stuff, it's a completely different story.

We started getting more clients and we were doing fine. It quickly became a fast-growing business. We were keeping busy all the time, which was great. In terms of marketing, we were getting some business from the SEO work I had done, but mainly it was pay-per-click to get customers. That started off really great, too, but then the more we did it, the less effective it became. I don't know why – perhaps there was more competition and it was costing us more to acquire a customer. It was costing us about $50 per customer, and that was quite a lot. It's okay if it's a repeat customer, but for a one-time customer, it was a little bit too much.

We were desperately looking for something else. Right about that time I became aware of authority positioning and being able to use those logos like ABC, CBS, FOX as trust triggers to put on your website. I had to convince my wife about the concept. It was really her business; she just kind of roped me in. I was trying to convince her to spend this money to get featured and be positioned better. She just didn't want to do it. I think it cost around $6,000 at the time. We were spending about $300 dollars a week on advertising and pay-per-click. She just didn't think it was worth it but I said, "This is something we're going to do once. We're going to be positioned better, and hopefully we're going to be able to attract a better kind of client and more of the kind of client that we want."

It's something you look at and you can see the value of it. Because I've got that marketing mind, I thought that this was something that I think will really make a difference, and it did. We went ahead purchased it.

We were interviewed for an article; the press release was written and we got our business featured in all these different publications. It made a tremendous difference to the business. I would say it was the real change in our business that happened almost overnight.

Can you take us step-by-step through what happened? So you signed on for $6,000 dollars as a client then you were interviewed for something or a press release was written? How did that start out?

Neil Howe: Yes, it was just a press release that was published to the major media channels. I was able to use those logos on my website.

What was the topic of the release? Was it that you opened the business or was it something specific that were doing in the business? What was the focus of the release?

Neil Howe: We were after certain clientele. We have seven kids and my wife doesn't like any chemical products or anything like that in the home. We wanted to be an all-natural cleaning service. We didn't use any chemicals in the cleaning, so that was the angle. This was a few years ago, and it's becoming more popular now.

We were just trying to educate on the dangers of some of the toxic chemicals that most people have in their house so that was the angle of the article.

We put the logos on our website. To get back into the figures, I was saying that it cost about $50 to acquire a customer. Right away, when I put those logos on the website, it went from $50 down to about $30.

Wow, so you had a real decrease.

Neil Howe: Yeah, that was a 40% saving on our advertising. At $300 dollars a week, that's $15,000 dollars a year we were spending on advertising. To save 40% on that was a $6,000-dollar savings just in a year.

You put the logos on your site, the seen on CBS, NBC, ABC, Wall Street Journal, etc. Did you do anything else with the release? Did you post the release on your site? Did you talk about it in social media? Did you contact your local media at all with the release? How else did you use that?

Neil Howe: To be honest, I didn't really do a great deal with it other than post it up on our website. I just threw the article out there, and I didn't really do much locally with it. I think the big difference that happened was when I put the logos up and people got to the site, they stayed around. They saw the energies of those trust triggers, those media logos, and they hung around for a little bit. They stayed on our site for a little bit longer. They read some of our stories. They looked into our pricing, and we were getting more calls.

When I talk about those trust triggers, this was the amazing thing to me. We'd get calls from people that would call us up, give us all their credit card information, leave us the keys to their house and just basically give us payment and free range of their house without ever checking us out. This was for a brand-new customer. This is not somebody that we've met or seen regularly. That never happened before we put those trust triggers on it.

It just goes to show you that people see those, and they're thinking to themselves, "Well, if they've been featured on these kinds of media outlets, then obviously they can be trusted." That made them willing to give out their credit card information and everything else.

How much time elapsed between the time you put those trust triggers on your website and the increase in your client base?

Neil Howe: Oh, it was almost overnight. In fact, I told you about the savings on pay-per-click, but we continued pay-per-click for only another month after that. We got to the point to where we had enough business to keep us going, and the SEO that we had helped us be found online with just the basic searches. So, we were still getting traffic to the website that way and we just found that people were calling us and calling us. We kept on booking jobs without paying for any more advertising.

That was about 2 1/2 years ago now. Other than the first month that I continued with the pay-per-click, I haven't spent another dime on advertising since.

That's amazing! So, you already had your traffic generation strategy in place between the SEO optimization and the pay-per-click. The difference became that once somebody got to your site, you suddenly became unique among all the other house cleaning agencies that folks were looking at. You became unique and different and immediately a respected authority in terms of what people were looking for so out of the 15 or 20 results somebody might get if they looked up Atlanta house cleaning. Your company stood head and above your competition once they landed on your site.

Neil Howe: Yeah and the other great thing that happened was when we first started out, like any job, it was a good job. When you're going into somebody's house it's not the most glamorous of jobs. We went into some bad neighborhoods and some bad places that you wouldn't want to go into. During the day was bad enough but to go there at night, you wouldn't even step foot in these neighborhoods. We went to some seedy places to start, with but what happened when we put those logos on the site as well, we positioned ourselves differently. We raised our prices outside the reach for many of those jobs that we didn't really want to do. We started attracting a different kind of audience as well. Instead of hitting those suburbs or any others in the city that were low income and they just wanted anybody to clean, we positioned ourselves better and started attracting a higher level of income. Those are the kind of clients where it only takes a few of them to keep us busy.

We're now working with doctors and lawyers. We've done a bunch of famous celebrities. Atlanta's getting bigger in the movie scene, as well.

We're attracting a lot of producers from movie shows. They just know those logos and they are comfortable with those logos and they call us often. Like I said, we're certainly not the cheapest, by far, in the industry. We're one of the most expensive, but we're now attracting the kind of audience that we want to be working with.

It sounds like through authority positioning, you've gotten yourself out of the situation of going with just anybody as a client to being much more discriminatory and really focusing on higher-level clients. They are the kind of client with whom you enjoy working, and my guess would be then that you had the freedom to turn down jobs that you previously didn't feel like you could turn down.

Neil Howe: Yeah that's right. When you think about our business and you're talking about some of the higher-end clients, they're very careful about who they have in their home.

Without doing a background check, they just feel comfortable by going to our website. Then obviously when we're going to meet them, you've got to present yourself well and do a good job. When you're cleaning people's houses, all their treasures are in their house. One of our latest clients had probably $100,000 dollars' worth of watches just sitting on their counter. Those people are paying for the comfort and the security of somebody that they know that they can trust. They're willing to pay more for that kind of level of service -- to have that knowledge that their stuff is safe and it's not going to be stolen or anything like that. They're willing to pay a little bit more for that experience and that luxury, whereas if you're just hiring anybody, you're not really sure what you're going to get.

If you're going into someone's house and if they happen to be a celebrity of sorts, celebrities are ripped off all the time by people who are going through their trash or cleaning their house or serving as their assistant or whatever and revealing things about their lifestyle that the celebrity doesn't want known. Whether it's something innocuous like this person eats a pound of chocolate a day to some really weird sex habit, the celebrity doesn't want anybody to know about it. Then, as somebody going into their home to clean it, you run across those things just inadvertently because of the nature of the work that you do.

Neil Howe: Yeah that's very true. We've seen a lot from a lot of different kinds of people. People leave their financial information lying about, and they leave all sorts of stuff lying out for people to see that they wouldn't otherwise. If there were guests coming over, that stuff wouldn't be lying out, but when the cleaning company comes over, I guess people just get used to it. They do put their trust in you, which is a good thing if you're trustworthy.

You talked about how you quit doing any pay-per-click advertising shortly after this media release came out about you and now you're getting referrals to other clients that are your ideal client. Are people making the referrals based on the fact that they can trust you from the media release or the good work that you did? Or is it some combination of both?

Neil Howe: It's probably a combination. I think if people are sending others to our site, then immediately when they get there, they're going to see those logos as well and it makes it a little easier for us to be referred. Mainly, I would say because the personality that we have. We take the time to get to know our customers and talk to them. They feel comfortable with us and that goes a long way. Our clients are comfortable enough to refer their friends and family who are also looking for the same kind of service.

So, as a result of this authority positioning that you have achieved, what does your wife say now about that investment?

Neil Howe: Thankfully, we did it early on in the business. It wasn't something that we waited years and years to do. We decided right away to position ourselves as the natural eco-cleaners. Our transition went from trying to just get anybody to realize we really need to be looking at the high-income level person and target them. It was definitely a very worthwhile investment and one that we're both glad that we made right at the start of the business. As I said, the change was almost overnight in the perception of our company.

Do you feel like your company, you and your wife have become local celebrities as a result of that authority positioning that was done for your company?

Neil Howe: I don't know if I would exactly say local celebrities, but it's nice not to be questioned about price. When people went website before we did the authority positioning, this was a fairly big problem. We'd give our price and they'd say, "I don't want to pay that much. Can you do it for this amount?" We would respond, "No, this is our price." At that point, the conversation completely ended. Now, we don't have to haggle about pricing -- our listed price is the price. If you want to pay it, great. If you can afford to pay it, then we're still talking. We don't really get those calls anymore from those ones that can't afford to pay it. I wouldn't exactly say we're celebrities, but we're well-liked by our customers and we're appreciated by them. We're certainly able to pick and choose who we want to work with.

It sounds like you have clients chasing you down and you stopped the client chase. You have clients just effortlessly approaching you based on the good work you've done. Of course, this wouldn't have been possible had you not provided a great service and had really great customer service. Authority positioning alone doesn't work if your clients feel completely hoodwinked or disappointed in the kind of service you have, but you've kept up that part of the agreement in terms of providing great service, great quality, great customer service and therefore got lots of referrals. You've become the hunted, rather than being the hunter I guess you could say.

Neil Howe: You've got to have substance. It's okay to be positioned in something but if you're not able to follow through and provide the service that you say you have or that's been said about you, then it's not going to work. You've got to have substance and be able to deliver. We're in a position now to where we can either grow and hire more people, or we're almost thinking about selling the business since there's something to sell. It is in a place where it's positioned, and somebody can take over a high-dollar clientele, a high-value customer. Many of our customers are worth $7,000-$9,000 dollars a year in revenue. It's given us an asset to think about selling, as well, because of the positioning.

Have you employed any other authority positioning strategies since then? Have you had another media releases published? Written a book? Gone for some interviews on podcasts, radio or TV stations?

Neil Howe: No, not really. I've got other businesses, as well and like I said, this started out as a part-time thing to make a few extra dollars and turned into a full-time six-figure business that we weren't really expecting. So we're kind of trying to even offload it, but the customers that we have right now are all fairly special people because we've developed relationships with them. It's hard to cut it loose.

At the same time, we're turning down hundreds of dollars of business every week just because we don't have the capacity to serve them. Now we've got a choice to make right now. We can either hire people to provide the same kind of service that we can ourselves or we offload it to somebody else who is going to be able to take the name and the positioning. That's kind of where we are.

That's a nice position to be in, to get to the point where you either need to grow or sell off the business because you're turning down viable customers or viable leads.

Neil Howe: It would be a problem if I were still paying for advertising, but like I said, I haven't paid a dime in over two years for advertising, so yes there's certainly money on the table that we could have if we wanted to go that next step and hire people to take over the business, which is probably what we're going to do in the foreseeable future.

With your success with your own cleaning business in terms of using the authority positioning to really elevate yourself among your competition in your local area, have you thought about striking out and working with other cleaning companies in other areas and talk to them about what you did and how they might be able to achieve success in their local area as you did?

Neil Howe: That's definitely something that's crossed our minds. We haven't taken action on that yet, but we have had tremendous results with our own company within the market, so that would be very easy to share that kind of example to other cleaning businesses, too.

It sounds like there might be some opportunities there to add on consulting and working with other cleaning company owners to help them replicate the kind of success you had.

Neil Howe: Yes, that's certainly something to think about. That's all a time commitment. That's one of the biggest problems I have right now -- being able to manage my time to take on different kinds of ventures.

Neil, as you look back on your experience with authority positioning, what advice would you give to an entrepreneur, whether they're in the cleaning business or some other business, who has the opportunity to put some authority positioning into place for his or her business around the media releases or the interviews in particular? What would you tell them if they're at that decision point?

Neil Howe: Oh, do it. There's no doubt in my mind that the best decision we could have made for our business was getting out the positioning. What would we be doing right now if I hadn't done it? It's a hard job, but when you're getting paid $50 - $100 dollars an hour, it makes it a little bit easier. If you're getting paid $10 or $15 dollars an hour, it's a different story. Being positioned is the best and that's what people are looking for.

Plus, having the added value thereof people seeking you to work with you as opposed to you having to go out and prospect for clients. You don't have to have those nit-picking conversations anymore about price because people are just giving you their credit card information and their house key right off the bat and want you to get started right away. Those are the things you can't really put a price on as a business owner.

Neil Howe: No, you can't. It's a great feeling knowing that you can turn down business -- it's a great problem to have. If we don't feel like the job is something that we want to do or we don't think we are going to get paid what we're worth, then we just say no. There are other companies out there that they can go and find, but if we're going to do the work, we're going to get paid what we think we're valued at.

Neil, thanks a bunch for the interview. Is there anything else you would like to add that I haven't asked about that has helped you build this cleaning company through using authority positioning?

Neil Howe: No, I think the basic thing that you covered was "just do it." Take the chance and see what it can do for your business. The second important thing is to make sure that you're giving value to you clientele because ultimately if it's not worth it, they're not going to pay. But there's a lot of people who are willing to pay a lot of money for the services that you can offer if it is valuable to them.

Bonuses for Readers

Remember, as a bonus for my readers, I have several bonuses that you can download at https://www.LocalCelebrityBranding.com/.

About Donna Gunter

Donna Gunter, Amazon #1 best-selling author of *Biz Smart Quick Guide: 10 Strategies to Online Visibility for More Traffic, Clicks and Profit!* and *Brand Yourself as the Trusted Local Celebrity^{TM}* helps entrepreneurs, consultants, speakers, coaches and professionals stop the client chase by leveraging their knowledge to gain authority status in their industry, then dramatically amplify their message and shows them how to convert the new audience into high-paying customers.

Using her proven *Become Business Famous* signature seven-step system, she works together with her clients to build powerful personal brands and grow their businesses through speaking, publishing and publicity.

WEBSITE: http://www.bizsmartmedia.com

FACEBOOK: https://www.facebook.com/BizSmartMedia

TWITTER: https://twitter.com/donnagunter

LINKEDIN: https://www.linkedin.com/in/donnagunter

www.ingramcontent.com/pod-product-compliance
Lightning Source LLC
Chambersburg PA
CBHW031427210526
45464CB00005B/2083